MW01226626

PRE - SCI/
Angele

The *Oxford Progressive English Readers* series provides a wide range of reading for learners of English.

Each book in the series has been written to follow the strict guidelines of a syllabus, wordlist and structure list. The texts are graded according to these guidelines; Grade 1 at a 1,400 word level, Grade 2 at a 2,100 word level, Grade 3 at a 3,100 word level, Grade 4 at a 3,700 word level and Grade 5 at a 5,000 word level.

The latest methods of text analysis, using specially designed software, ensure that readability is carefully controlled at every level. Any new words which are vital to the mood and style of the story are explained within the text, and reoccur throughout for maximum reinforcement. New language items are also clarified by attractive illustrations.

Each book has a short section containing carefully graded exercises and controlled activities, which test both global and specific understanding.

Stories from Shakespeare's Histories

Retold by Katherine Mattock

1994
Hong Kong
Oxford University Press
Oxford Singapore Tokyo

Oxford University Press

Oxford   New York
Athens   Auckland   Bangkok   Bombay
Calcutta   Cape Town   Dar es Salaam   Delhi
Florence   Hong Kong   Istanbul   Karachi
Kuala Lumpur   Madras   Madrid   Melbourne
Mexico City   Nairobi   Paris   Singapore
Taipei   Tokyo   Toronto

and associated companies in
Berlin   Ibadan

Oxford is a trade mark of Oxford University Press

First published 1994
1   3   5   7   9   10   8   6   4   2

Retold by Katherine Mattock
Illustrated by Wu Siu Kau
Syllabus designer: David Foulds
Text analysis by Luxfield Consultants Ltd

ISBN 0 19 586307 0

Printed in Hong Kong
Published by Oxford University Press (Hong Kong) Ltd
18/F Warwick House, Taikoo Place, 979 King's Road,
Quarry Bay, Hong Kong

CONTENTS

HENRY THE FOURTH, PART I: HENRY'S PROBLEMS

Trouble in the land

Henry Bolingbroke was crowned Henry the Fourth, King of England, in the year 1399. He was of royal blood — a Plantagenet, a grandson of King Edward the Third, and the son of John of Gaunt who had been Duke of Lancaster. But he took the throne from his cousin, King Richard the Second, who had sent him abroad and not allowed him to return. Henry felt guilty, and his reign was troubled from the beginning.

Many nobles had supported him when he returned from France to claim his father's title, but they turned against him after he became king and Richard was murdered. Henry's eldest son, the Prince of Wales, was also called Henry, but his friends called him Harry or Hal. He led a wild life and the king worried that he was not fit to be heir to the throne. There was civil war in the kingdom. And then, when Henry hoped for peace at home so that he could lead an expedition to the Holy Land, there was trouble on the borders between England, Wales and Scotland.

25

From the west, news came to him at the Palace of Westminster that a Welshman called Owen Glendower had defeated an English army under Edmund Mortimer, the Earl of March. 'Mortimer is a prisoner, and 1,000 of his men of Herefordshire have been killed, my lord,' reported the Earl of Westmoreland.

From the north came news that Harry Percy, known as 'Hotspur', the fiery son of the Earl of Northumberland, had fought the Scots under the Earl of Douglas, and won. 'I saw 10,000 Scotsmen lying in their own blood,' reported Sir Walter Blunt, 'and Hotspur took many prisoners.'

This second battle was a victory for England, but the king could not enjoy it. His eldest son, as usual, was not at the court. 'Lucky Northumberland,' he sighed, 'to have such an honourable son, while my young Harry lives a life of shame. I'd willingly exchange my Harry Plantagenet for his Harry Percy! This young Percy is too proud, however. He won't give his prisoners to me, his king!'

Westmoreland also said that Hotspur was being encouraged by his uncle, the Earl of Worcester. 'Worcester is against you, my lord,' he said.

'I've sent for the Percys,' announced the king. 'They must come and explain themselves to my council.'

No ransom for Mortimer

Worcester, Northumberland and Hotspur arrived, and were told by the king that they had become too proud. Worcester replied that Henry had only got the throne with their help. The king was angry. Hotspur had refused to give him his prisoners unless the king paid a ransom to get back Glendower's prisoner, Mortimer. Mortimer was Hotspur's wife's brother. He had led the

English army, but now he had married Glendower's daughter. The king shouted:

'You should give me your prisoners, and forget about Mortimer. I won't pay money for a traitor to England. Let the rebel die on the Welsh mountains!' 5

'Rebel? Mortimer is no rebel, my lord,' protested Hotspur. 'He's loyal and true. He fought hard against Glendower, man to man, across the River Severn.'

'He never fought Glendower,' declared the king. 'Don't speak to me about Mortimer — and send me 10 your Scottish prisoners. Lord Northumberland, you and your son may leave. But send me those prisoners.'

The Percys plot against the king

Harry Percy and Northumberland were now alone.

'I won't send the king my prisoners!' said Hotspur. 15 'I'll follow him and say so.'

'Are you mad?' asked his father. 'Stop to think.'

'But the king orders me not to speak about Mortimer!' argued Hotspur. 'I will speak about him. I'll fight for him. I'll raise him as high as this ungrateful 20 Bolingbroke!' The Earl of Worcester now returned. 'The king wants all my prisoners,' Hotspur informed his uncle, 'and he is afraid to hear the name of Mortimer!'

'I'm not surprised,' said Worcester. 'Didn't King Richard the Second name Mortimer as heir to the 25 throne?'

'He did,' agreed Northumberland. 'I heard him myself, before he went to Ireland — shortly before he was deposed, had the throne taken from him, and was murdered.' 30

'So that's why his cousin, the king, would like Mortimer to die on the Welsh mountains!' said Hotspur. 'But what about us? You two (God forgive you!) helped to depose Richard and crown this ungrateful Henry. Will you now let him turn against you? There's still time to save yourselves. I say —'

'Say no more, nephew,' interrupted Worcester. 'I'll tell
5 you my dangerous plan.'

'What does danger matter,' demanded Hotspur, 'if there's honour to be won? By heaven, I'd fetch bright honour from the moon or the bottom of the sea ...'

'Good nephew, let me speak. Those Scots who are
10 your prisoners —'

'I'll keep them all,' threatened the fiery Hotspur. 'By God, the king won't have one of them. He won't ransom Mortimer and he ordered me not to speak about Mortimer! But I will! I'll shout "Mortimer" in his ear! I'll
15 defy this Bolingbroke and that no-good Prince of Wales! I'd kill the prince with one of his own drinking-pots, if I didn't think that his father might be pleased!'

'You're an impatient fool!' said Northumberland.

'But this Bolingbroke is hateful!' shouted Hotspur.
20 'Such a king of smiles he was, before he got the crown. I was "gentle Harry Percy" and "kind cousin" then ...'

At last Hotspur allowed his uncle to speak. 'Go back to your Scottish prisoners,' Worcester advised him, 'and return them home without any ransom. That should
25 persuade the Earl of Douglas to support us. Meanwhile,' he told Northumberland, 'you go to Richard Scroop, the Archbishop of York, and persuade him to support us too. He already hates Bolingbroke ...'

'A noble plot!' cried Hotspur. 'So Scotland and York
30 will join with Mortimer?'

'Yes,' Worcester replied, 'and we must work fast, to save our own heads. The king will never trust us because he thinks we want to be repaid for helping him get the throne. He's already beginning to treat us
35 as strangers.'

'Yes,' exclaimed Hotspur, 'and we'll be revenged on him!'

'Don't do anything unless I tell you to,' said Worcester quickly. 'When the time is right, I'll go to Glendower and Mortimer in Wales, and arrange for you and Douglas to join us with all our forces.'

So the father and son returned to the north to do as Worcester had told them. 'Let the battle come soon!' cried Hotspur.

'Sweet Hal'

The Prince of Wales was not at the court. He was enjoying himself with his fat old drinking companion, Sir John Falstaff.

'Now, Hal, what time of day is it, lad?' asked Falstaff sleepily.

'What do you care?' laughed Harry. 'You're so drunk that you're asleep half the day.'

'Perhaps you're right, Hal. Those of us who steal purses tell the time by the moon and the stars, not the sun … But, I beg you, sweet prince, when you're king, don't hang thieves.'

'I won't,' agreed Harry. 'You will.'

Falstaff was pleased. 'You mean I'll be the judge? I'll be a splendid judge.'

'No, I mean you'll do the hanging!'

'You're the rudest, wickedest sweet young prince!' declared the knight. 'You could ruin the innocence of a saint, and you've certainly ruined me!'

'Why, do I ever ask you to pay for anything?'

'No, I admit that — but before I knew you, Hal, I was an innocent man, and now I'm wicked. I must give up this life, and I will give it up. I won't be damned for any king's son …'

Harry smiled, 'And where shall we steal a purse tomorrow, Jack?'

'Anywhere you like, Hal,' cried Falstaff. 'I'll be there!' At this moment, their friend Ned Poins came in to join them, looking pleased with himself. 'Ah, here's Poins,' said the knight. 'He'll tell us where the next robbery will be.'

'Good morning, Ned,' said the prince.

'Good morning, sweet Hal. Good drinking, Sir John?' said Ned Poins. 'Well, it's all fixed, lads — tomorrow morning early, four o'clock, Gad's Hill in Kent! There'll be rich men riding to Canterbury and traders with fat purses riding to London. I have masks to hide our faces. You have horses. It'll be easy! We'll be back in London by tomorrow night, with purses full of gold. I've already ordered supper in Eastcheap.'

Falstaff looked at the prince. 'Will you come, Hal?'

'I rob? I a thief?' Harry was all innocence. 'Not I, I'll stay at home.'

'Then I'll be a traitor when you're king!' growled Falstaff.

Poins asked Falstaff to leave him alone with the prince. 'I'll persuade him, Sir John,' he said.

'Good,' said Falstaff. 'Then I'll go to Eastcheap, to the tavern.'

Poins has a trick

As Falstaff departed, Poins began to whisper to Harry, 'My good sweet lord, ride with us tomorrow. I have a trick to play on Falstaff, but I can't manage it alone... Listen, this is it. Falstaff, Bardolph and some of the others will rob the travellers — and then you and I will rob Falstaff and Bardolph.'

'But how can we get away from them to do that?' The prince was doubtful.

'Easy! We'll set out before or after them, and fail to meet them as arranged. Then they'll do the robbery themselves — and as soon as they've finished, we'll attack them.'

'But they'll recognize our horses and clothes and —'

'No, they won't. I'll tie our horses out of sight, and bring some disguise to put on over our usual clothes.'

'Won't they be too strong for us?'

'No, they're all cowards! And the the best thing about the joke will be the lies that the fat rogue will tell us at supper. How he fought with thirty men or more! What blows he suffered...!'

Harry laughed and gave in. 'I'll go with you, Ned. You provide everything we'll need — and we'll have supper tomorrow night at the tavern in Eastcheap.'

But when Poins too had left, the prince looked thoughtful.

'I know what you're like, my friends,' he said to himself, 'and I'll go along with your idle nonsense for a while. I'm not yet like Harry Percy, the Hotspur of the north, who kills a hundred Scots before breakfast, washes his hands and says to his wife, "Damn this quiet life!" But soon I'll stop all this bad behaviour. I'll be like the sun breaking through grey clouds — I'll seem more splendid for the sudden change...'

HENRY THE FOURTH, PART I: ROBBERS AND REBELS

The robbery at Gad's Hill

By four o'clock next morning, the prince and Poins were at Gad's Hill. So were Falstaff, Bardolph and two other companions.

5 'Poins! Poins! Where's Poins, Hal?' called Falstaff in the dark.

The prince told him that Poins had walked to the top of the hill.

'The rogue has taken my horse and I don't know
10 where he's tied it. You know that I can't walk far! Give me my horse!'

'Be quiet, Fat-belly!' said the prince. 'Lie down with your ear close to the ground and then listen for the travellers!'

15 Falstaff refused, saying he would never be able to get up again. As they argued, Bardolph came up and urged them to put on their masks. 'There are some riders coming over the hill! They look like men with money! Eight or ten of them.'

20 'Then you four meet them here in the narrow lane,' the prince ordered quietly. 'Ned Poins and I will wait lower down, so that if they escape from you, they'll run into us.'

'Oh dear!' The knight was nervous.

25 'What, Sir John the Fat, are you a coward?' demanded Harry.

'I know I'm fat like John of Gaunt, your grandfather, but I'm not a coward, Hal,' replied Falstaff.

'We'll see,' said Harry as the riders approached.

Now Poins came forward. 'Sir John, your horse is up
the hill behind the tree when you need it. We two are
going now. Good luck!' Quickly, Poins and Harry
disappeared, to put on their disguises.

'Right, lads,' said Falstaff to the others. 'Are you   5
ready? Here we go!'

The riders, as they came near, got off their horses to
lead them down the steep part of the hill and stretch
their own legs.

'Stop! Give us your money!' shouted the thieves   10
suddenly.

'Down with them! Cut their throats, the rich villains!'
shouted Falstaff. 'Take their gold!'

Between them, the four thieves robbed the travellers
and bound them.   15

'Come, lads,' said Falstaff. 'Let's share out the gold
between us and be on our horses before sunrise. The
prince and Poins are cowards! There's no more courage
in that Poins than in a wild duck. I say that we four
keep the money for ourselves.'   20

As the thieves were emptying the purses, the prince
and Poins, both now disguised, came back and attacked
them.

'Oh! Oh! Oh!' Bardolph and his friends ran away
immediately.   25

'Ow! Aah! Ow!' roared Falstaff. After a blow or two,
he ran away also, as fast as his fat legs would carry
him, leaving all the money behind.

'Well, that was easy!' smiled Harry as Poins picked
up the money. 'Let's go merrily back to London, good   30
Ned! The thieves have gone off in all directions, and
Falstaff's sweating so much that he waters the earth as
he walks! If I wasn't laughing so much, I think I'd pity
him.'

'How the fat rogue roared!' said Poins.   35

Back in Eastcheap

The prince and Poins rode straight back to London to have supper at the tavern in Eastcheap, and to wait for Falstaff. Finally the knight arrived, tired and thirsty.

'Old Sir John's at the door with some friends, my lord,' announced the hostess of the tavern, Mistress Quickly.

The prince told her to call him in, and Falstaff entered, followed by Bardolph and the other thieves.

'Welcome, Jack!' Poins greeted him. 'Where have you been?'

'Damn all cowards!' exclaimed the knight, calling for wine. 'There are only three or four good men left in England — and one of them is fat and grows old! It's a bad world.'

'What's the matter, Fat-belly? What are you muttering?' asked the prince.

'A king's son, you?' Falstaff was scornful. 'You're a coward. You too, Poins.

I'd give a thousand pounds if I could run as fast as you.'
The knight stopped as Poins put his hand on his dagger.
'Damn all cowards, I still say,' he muttered.

Harry looked serious. 'What's the matter?' he repeated,
as the knight wiped his lips and called for more wine.

'There are four of us here who took a thousand
pounds this morning,' said Falstaff.

'Then where's the money, Jack?' asked Harry.

'Taken from us again. A hundred men against us poor
four.'

'A hundred?'

'I swear that I fought twelve of them myself. I'm lucky
to be alive,' claimed the knight. 'Look at my sword!' He
drew out a sword that was cut almost through. 'Still, I
fought well. Ask Bardolph.'

The prince told Bardolph to describe what had
happened.

'We four attacked about twelve men —' Bardolph
began.

'We attacked sixteen or more, my lord,' Falstaff
interrupted.

'— and tied them,' Bardolph went on. 'Then, as we
were sharing out the money, six or seven other men
attacked us —'

'— and untied the rest, and then all the others came,'
said Falstaff quickly.

Harry asked Falstaff if he had fought with them all.

'Fifty or more. Fifty-three of them on poor old Jack,
I swear,' answered the knight.

'I pray to God you didn't murder any of them.'

Falstaff said that he had indeed killed two of the men
who attacked him. Then he said that four men had
attacked him. Then he increased the number to seven,
then nine, then eleven; and he claimed to have killed
seven of the eleven.

'Eleven men grown out of two!' exclaimed the prince.

Falstaff was enjoying his story. 'And then in the dark, Hal — it was so dark, I couldn't see my own hand — three men in green attacked me from behind —'

5   But Harry had heard enough. 'Lies, a mountain of lies, you mountain of a man!' he declared. 'How could you know, when it was so dark, that the men wore green? You're a coward, you great meat-hill! Now you listen to me.'

10 'Listen well, Jack,' advised Poins.

'My story,' said Harry, 'is short and plain. We two saw you four attack four travellers and bind them and rob them of their money. Then we two attacked you four, took the money — and can show it to you here, in this
15 house.'

Falstaff was silent, but the prince showed no mercy. 'And you, Falstaff,' he continued, 'just roared and ran away. What a knave, to claim that your sword was cut in a fight! Shame on you! What story, what excuse are
20 you going to give us now?'

'Let's hear, Jack,' said Poins. 'What excuse?'

Falstaff thought quickly. 'I knew you all the time, my masters!' he declared. 'I knew you, but I couldn't kill the heir to the throne, could I? I'm as brave as a lion,
25 but even a lion won't touch a true prince ... Er, anyway, lads, hearts of gold, I'm glad you have the money! Let's be merry! Shall we do a play?'

'Yes,' agreed Harry. 'A play about running away!'

News from the king

30 They were interrupted by Mistress Quickly, who ran in to say that a nobleman had arrived from the court. 'He wants to speak to you, my lord the prince! He says he comes from your father.'

Harry refused to see the nobleman. Falstaff offered to go instead, and while the knight was out of the room, the prince questioned the other thieves. 'So you're all lions too?' he asked. 'You ran away because you wouldn't hurt the true prince?'   5

'I ran because the others ran,' admitted Bardolph.

'And how did Falstaff's sword get so cut about?'

'He cut it with his own dagger,' admitted another thief, 'and said he would make you believe it was done in the fight. He persuaded us to do the same.'   10

'Yes,' agreed Bardolph, 'and to push stiff grass up our noses so that they bled, and then to spread the blood on our clothes and swear that it was the blood of other men. I blushed with shame at his tricks.'

'Bardolph, you villain!' exclaimed the prince. 'You've   15
been blushing for eighteen years, ever since you stole your first drink.' (Bardolph's nose and face were always red, as everyone knew.) 'Ah, here comes poor, thin Jack!'

But Falstaff had serious news to report from the   20
palace. The king had learned that the Percys were joining forces against him with Glendower, Mortimer, the Earl of Douglas and a thousand Scots ...

'Your father's beard has turned white at the news,' Falstaff informed the prince, 'and you must go to the   25
court in the morning ... You have those devils, Douglas, Percy and Glendower as enemies! Aren't you afraid, Hal?'

'Not I!' Harry laughed. 'I'm not a lion like you!'

'But you'll be in trouble tomorrow when you see the   30
king. You'd better practise your answers.'

'Then we'll do a play, as you wanted,' replied Harry. 'You can pretend to be my father and ask me about my life.'

'Right!' smiled Falstaff.   35

A play at the tavern

The knight went over to a large chair with a cushion
on it. 'This chair can be my throne and this cushion,
my crown,' he said. 'And the king must speak in sorrow,
5 so bring me some wine to make my eyes look red…'

'King Henry' put on his 'crown' and
sat down on his 'throne'. Mistress
Quickly and the others clapped.

'Oh, wonderful!' cried Mistress
Quickly. 'Look at Sir John's serious
face! Just like a real actor!'

'*Harry,*' Falstaff declared,
'*you waste your time in bad
places with bad people. Shall
the King of England's son be
a thief and steal purses? I
speak to you in tears and
sorrow… And yet there is
one good man whom I have
often seen in your company,
though I don't know his name.*'

'*What sort of man, Your
Majesty?*' asked the prince,
standing before him.

25 '*A good, large man, with a cheerful look and a most
noble bearing,*' said the knight. '*His age, fifty or perhaps
sixty. And, I remember now, his name is Falstaff.
Harry, I swear there is goodness in this man. Keep him,
send away the rest… Now tell me, you naughty lad,*
30 *where have you been for the last month?*'

Harry protested that Falstaff was not speaking like a
king. 'Change places,' he ordered. 'I'll play my father.'

'You're deposing me?' grumbled Falstaff. 'He won't
be half as good,' he told the audience.

'*Now, Harry,*' the new 'King Henry' began, putting the cushion on his head, '*where have you come from?*'

'*My noble lord, from Eastcheap,*' Falstaff replied, standing now before the 'throne'.

'*I receive dreadful complaints about your behaviour,*' said Harry.   5

'*By god, my lord, they're false!*' shouted Falstaff. 'I'll show you acting!' he told the audience.

'*There's a devil in the shape of a fat old man who is your companion,*' Harry continued. '*Why do you* 10 *spend your time with that wine-pot, that great belly, that villain? What is he good for, except to drink, eat and tell lies?*'

'*But whom does Your Majesty mean?*' asked Falstaff.

'*That old villain, Falstaff,*' said Harry.   15

'*I, er, know the man,*' said Falstaff.

'*I know you do!*' replied Harry.

'*But there's no more harm in him than in myself!*' protested the knight. '*Is it a sin to be old and merry? If wine is a fault, God help the truly wicked! And if* 20 *it's wrong to be fat… No, my good lord: send away Poins, Bardolph and the rest, but sweet Jack Falstaff, kind Jack Falstaff, brave old Jack Falstaff, don't send him from Harry's company. If you send big Jack away, you send away all the world!*'   25

'*I do,*' said the prince, serious for a moment. '*I will.*'

Officers of the law

Suddenly, there was a loud knocking at the door. Mistress Quickly ran out, followed by Bardolph.

'Oh, my lord, my lord!' cried Bardolph, running back. 30 'There are officers of the law at the door!'

'Out, you rogue!' said the knight. 'Don't stop the play, Hal. I've still a lot to say about that Falstaff.'

'But they're coming into the house!' cried Mistress Quickly.

Harry told Falstaff to hide behind the curtain and the other men to go upstairs. 'Now for a serious face

5 indeed!' he said.

A sergeant entered. Some gentlemen had lost their purses in the robbery, he told the prince, and he was looking for the men responsible. One of them was a well-known man, who was huge and 'as fat as butter'.

'That man's not here, I assure you,' said the prince. 'He's doing something for me. But I'll send him to you tomorrow, Master Sergeant, I promise. If

15 he has robbed these men, he shall be punished for it.'

This satisfied the sergeant and, when he had gone, Harry looked around for Falstaff.

'Fast asleep behind the curtain, my lord!' announced Bardolph.

20 On Harry's orders, he emptied the knight's pockets and read out a tavern bill that he found there.

'Oh, wicked!' exclaimed the prince as he listened. 'Only a penny for bread, but five shillings for wine…! Well, let him sleep there till dawn. I must go to the

25 court in the morning. We'll all have to fight now, and I'll make this fat rogue commander of a company of foot-soldiers. Marching will kill him!'

3

HENRY THE FOURTH, PART I: PREPARING FOR WAR

Hotspur is impatient

The Earl of Worcester had now completed his plot to put Mortimer on the English throne. The rebels, as Falstaff had reported, were gathering their forces. They planned to meet with their armies at Shrewsbury on the River Severn; and both Worcester and his nephew Hotspur had gone to Glendower's castle to arrange it. 5

They were followed there by Hotspur's worried and loving wife.

'What is it that carries you away?' Lady Percy had cried as Hotspur prepared to leave their castle in Northumberland. 10

'Why, my horse, my love — my horse!' Harry Percy had replied with a laugh.

'You mad ape! I demand to know your business, Harry. I'll break your little finger, Harry,' she had warned him, 'if you won't tell me the truth. I fear that my brother Mortimer wants to claim the throne and has sent for you to help him.' 15

Lady Percy was right. In Wales, when she arrived, her brother and husband were studying a map with Glendower. They were dividing the kingdom between them. 20

'England south and east of the rivers Trent and Severn is mine,' announced Mortimer. 'Wales and all the lands west of the River Severn go to you, Owen Glendower,' he told his new father-in-law. 'And the rest of England, everything north of the River Trent, is yours, Harry Percy.' 25

But Hotspur did not like the division. His share wasn't as large as the other two, he protested. He wanted more.

'I won't allow it,' declared powerful Glendower.

5 'Won't you?' Hotspur's temper began to rise.

'No, I won't.'

'Who's going to stop me?'

'I am.'

Then Glendower decided not to quarrel any more,

10 and Hotspur stopped arguing, too.

Mortimer sighed. He had arranged to leave the next day with Worcester and Hotspur to go to Shrewsbury, to meet the Earls of Northumberland and Douglas. But suddenly, Hotspur decided, tomorrow was not soon

15 enough.

'Let's go now!' he cried.

'Yes, there's a bright moon, go!' said Glendower. His Welsh army was not yet ready. He said he would follow the English rebels as soon as possible, bringing Lady

20 Percy and his daughter, now Mortimer's wife.

Harry faces the king

In the end, Hotspur and Worcester went to Shrewsbury without either Mortimer or Glendower. Meanwhile, in London, the Prince of Wales went to the Palace of

25 Westminster. The king was angry that he had been away so long.

'God was punishing me for my sins,' King Henry cried in despair, 'when he gave me a son like you!' Harry's behaviour and his friends, he said, were bad.

30 One of his brothers had had to take his place on the king's council. Harry himself was almost a stranger to the court and the other princes.

'If I had behaved like you,' the king continued, 'if I had thrown myself before the public, kept such company, made myself so cheap — they would not have given me the throne: Richard the Second would still be king. But I, Bolingbroke, was seldom seen, while   5
Richard showed himself too much in the company of fools, so that the people grew tired of him.

'You are behaving now as Richard was then, when I returned from France. And Hotspur is behaving as I was then. Hotspur is more worthy of my throne than you   10
are. He's no older than you, he has no claim to the throne and yet he marches against the king, he leads lords and bishops into battle. He has won great honour already against Douglas — and now he has made a friend of him, and together they shake the peace and   15
safety of my throne! Percy, Douglas, Mortimer, the Archbishop of York, they're all preparing to fight against us … But why do I tell you this, Harry? You yourself are my nearest and dearest enemy.'

Harry had listened to his father almost in silence.   20
Now he began to answer, begging his father to forgive him for the faults of his youth.

'Your Majesty,' Harry declared, 'I shall, from now, be more worthy to be called your son. I shall wash away my shame with blood. I shall fight this brave, much-   25
honoured Hotspur. As I fight him, I will become glorious, like him, and so I will no longer sin. And his honour will become my honour. I promise you this in God's name!'

This change in his son greatly pleased the king and   30
he gave Harry an immediate military command. When it was announced that the English rebels had now met the Scottish Douglas at Shrewsbury, Henry gathered his own armies. There was one under his young son John of Lancaster, and the Earl of Westmoreland, one under   35

Harry, and one under himself. They were to meet at Shrewsbury in twelve days' time.

Falstaff gets a command

From the palace, Harry went to Eastcheap, to look for
5 Falstaff.

Sir John was drinking at the tavern with Bardolph. He had lost so much weight since the robbery, he declared, that his skin hung on him as loosely as an old lady's dress. 'I must repent and give up this
10 wickedness, my Knight of the Burning Lamp!' he said to the red-nosed Bardolph. 'I was good enough in the past, but now, I swear, I've forgotten what the inside of a church looks like! And keeping that nose of yours on fire by buying you drinks has made me poor.'

15 Mistress Quickly entered and Falstaff asked if she had found out who had stolen his money, 'Can't I even have a rest without someone emptying my pockets?'

'There are no thieves in this house,' said the woman. 'I know you, Sir John. You owe money here and you're
20 starting a quarrel to cheat me of it.' The knight owed twenty-four pounds for food and drink and money lent to him.

Falstaff said that it wasn't his fault, because the Prince of Wales owed him a thousand pounds. 'The prince is
25 a knave! If he was here, I'd beat him like a dog.'

As he said it, Harry marched in. 'Welcome, lad!' the knight declared without a pause. 'Do you know, Hal, the other night I fell asleep here behind the curtain and someone emptied my pockets? I lost over a hundred
30 pounds.'

'My lord, he's accusing me!' exclaimed Mistress Quickly. 'And he says that you're a knave, and that you owe him a thousand pounds.'

Harry looked at the knight. The knight smiled at him. 'A thousand pounds, Hal? No, a million! Your love is worth a million, and you owe me your love!'

'You great rogue!' declared Harry. 'You call me knave? You accuse an honest woman of stealing when there was nothing in your pockets except bills?'

'Ah,' said Falstaff, pleased, 'so you confess that you emptied my pockets! Hostess, I forgive you ... Now, Hal, tell me the news at court. How did you explain about the robbery?'

'All the money's been paid back,' Harry replied, to the knight's horror. He had made peace with his father, he said, but now they must all go to war. Falstaff, he added, must command a company of foot-soldiers.

'Foot, not horse-soldiers?' The knight's horror increased. 'I'd prefer horse!'

Harry shook his head and told Falstaff to come to him next day to get his orders and the money to carry them out. 'Bardolph,' he said, 'take these letters to the Earl of Westmoreland and my brother John ... The land is in disorder. Either we or Percy must fall.'

Bad news for the rebels

Hotspur, Worcester and Douglas were already at Shrewsbury when they received a message from Hotspur's father, the Earl of Northumberland. He was ill, the message said, and could not join them.

The news greatly disturbed Worcester. He was afraid people would think Northumberland did not support the rebellion.

Then Sir Richard Vernon arrived, announcing that Prince John and the Earl of Westmoreland were marching towards them, with 7,000 men. The king was also on his way.

'Where are the Prince of Wales and his careless companions?' said Hotspur.

'All coming to fight,' declared Vernon to the rebels' surprise, 'glittering in gold, as full of life as the month
5 of May and as splendid as the sun in summer. I saw young Harry, with his armour on, jump onto his horse so easily that —'

'No more!' interrupted Hotspur. 'Let them come. Harry to Harry, horse to horse, we'll meet, fight and never part until one of us drops dead ... I wish Glendower had arrived, though.'

But Vernon had not finished. On his way through Worcestershire, he had learned that Glendower could not get his army together for another two weeks. The king, he added, had 30,000 men altogether.

The rebels were all worried. But Hotspur exclaimed
25 boldly: 'Let the king have 40,000 men! We can fight them, even without my father and Glendower.'

The king offers peace

King Henry, Prince Harry and Prince John met near Shrewsbury with their men and set up their camp. Even
30 Falstaff and Bardolph had arrived, leading 150 poor soldiers.

Hotspur and Douglas wanted to attack immediately, that night, before the king's horses had rested.

Worcester and Vernon wanted to wait until all their own men and horses had arrived.

As the four rebels argued, Sir Walter Blunt came to them with the Earl of Westmoreland, bringing a message from King Henry. The king, he told Hotspur, admitted the great debt he owed to the Percys. He was willing to settle any arguments, and to pardon them and all the other rebels.

Hotspur was scornful. The king, he said, was a man who made promises but did not keep them.

'My father and my uncle and myself gave Henry Bolingbroke that crown he wears,' he informed Blunt. 'When he arrived back from France, my father Northumberland welcomed him. When he swore to God that he came back only to be Duke of Lancaster, my father believed and helped him. So the lords and people bowed to Bolingbroke. They met him in cities and villages, waited on bridges, stood in lanes, offered him presents and their trust. And then, as he began to feel his power, he broke his promise to my father and, while King Richard was away in Ireland, began to interfere in the government —'

Blunt tried to stop Hotspur, but could not.

'Soon after,' Hotspur continued wildly, 'Bolingbroke deposed Richard, then murdered him. Since then, he has refused to ransom his cousin Mortimer, who should be his king. He has shamed my victories, dismissed my uncle from the council, my father from the court… And that is why, to protect ourselves, we have started this rebellion. We no longer recognize Bolingbroke's title to the throne!'

Blunt asked if he should carry this reply to the king.

'No,' said Hotspur. 'Early tomorrow morning, my uncle Worcester will tell the king himself.'

HENRY THE FOURTH, PART I: THE BATTLE OF SHREWSBURY

'What is honour?'

The sun shone red at dawn the next day, as Worcester arrived with Vernon at the king's camp.

The king wanted to know why Worcester had
5 rebelled and brought them all to the edge of war.

Worcester said that it was the king's own fault, that Henry himself had caused the rebellion by turning against the Percys. 'We were the first and dearest of your friends,' he told Henry. 'It was myself, my brother
10 and his son who brought you home to England. You swore to us that you wanted only to claim your title as the Duke of Lancaster. But then you took advantage of Richard's absence in Ireland, seized the whole kingdom, forgot your promise and turned away from us. For our
15 own safety, we have been forced to lead this rebellion against you.'

'I've heard all this before!' said the king impatiently. 'You've announced it on the streets and in the churches. But rebels can always make their cause look good, and
20 there are always some people ready to listen…'

Suddenly, the Prince of Wales stepped forward and offered to fight Hotspur himself, if this would prevent a full battle. 'Tell your nephew,' he said to Worcester, 'that the Prince of Wales joins all the world in praise of
25 Harry Percy. There is no braver man alive, no man who has done more noble deeds, while I to my shame have played the fool. But here, before the king my father, I offer to meet Hotspur in a fight between the two of us, to save blood on both sides.'

The king then repeated his earlier offer to pardon all the rebels. If Percy accepted, the king would be friends with him and all his followers. But if Percy did not accept, the rebels would receive no mercy.

Worcester left for the rebel camp. 5

'He won't accept,' said Harry. 'Douglas and Hotspur think that they can fight the whole world!'

'So prepare for battle,' ordered the king. 'We shall attack as soon as we receive their answer. Our cause is just, may God protect us!' 10

He returned to his tent and Falstaff approached his old friend. 'Hal, if you see me down in the battle, will you protect me?'

'Say your prayers,' was Harry's short answer.

'I wish it was bedtime, Hal, and all was well.' 15

'You have to die some day!' exclaimed Harry.

'But not yet,' muttered the knight as the prince left him. 'I must fight. Honour demands it. But what is this "honour"? A word! Air! Can honour mend a broken arm or leg? No! Who has honour? Only the dead! Away! I 20 don't want any of it!'

Worcester hides the truth

Worcester, returning to the rebel camp, ordered Vernon not to tell Hotspur that Henry had repeated his offer of a pardon. The king would never keep his promise, he 25 claimed, and he would continue to doubt the Percys because they had been traitors. He might forgive Hotspur because he was young and fiery, but he would never forgive Northumberland and Worcester.

So Worcester announced that the king had challenged 30 the rebels to immediate battle, and Vernon stayed silent.

'Defy him!' cried Douglas. 'Let Westmoreland tell the King of England we accept his challenge!'

While Douglas went away to give that message to Westmoreland, Worcester continued to hide the truth.

'The king showed no mercy,' he told Hotspur.

'I hope you didn't ask for any!' exclaimed Hotspur.

5   'I told him gently of our complaints,' claimed Worcester, 'and he called us rebels and traitors...'

It was only after Douglas returned to report that Westmoreland had left for the king's camp with their answer, that Worcester mentioned the Prince of Wales's

10 challenge.

'I wish only the two of us needed to fight today!' cried Hotspur. 'Tell me, tell me! How did he announce it? Was he scornful?'

'No, indeed,' Vernon spoke for the first time. 'I never

15 in my life heard a challenge made more quietly. He praised you, and then rebuked himself for his past behaviour. I tell you, if the prince comes out of this battle alive, England has an heir to be proud of!'

Hotspur laughed. 'Here's a change! Well, no matter what Harry's like, I mean to put a soldier's arm around him before night!'

A messenger came up to say that the king was approaching fast.

'Good, then there's no time for my poor speeches,' smiled Hotspur, drawing his sword. 'Let each man do his best — and I'll make this sword red with the best blood I can find today... Sound the trumpets! Advance!'

The battle

So the king's army advanced towards the rebel camp
and the battle began.

To trick the rebels, several lords were disguised as
the king, and the Earl of Douglas killed three of them, 5
including the Earl of Stafford and Sir Walter Blunt.

'All's done, all's won!' Douglas cried to Hotspur,
pointing at Blunt's body. 'Here lies the king! — I know
him by his coat.'

'No, Douglas,' replied Hotspur, looking down. 'I 10
know this face well. This was the brave Sir Walter Blunt,
disguised to look like the king. The king has many men
disguised as him.'

'Then, by my sword, I'll kill all of them, one by one,'
shouted Douglas, 'until I meet the king himself!' 15

He and Hotspur ran back into the battle, as Falstaff
crept quietly away from it.

'Well,' the knight said to himself, 'my poor soldiers
are finished. There aren't three of my 150 left alive…
But who's this?' He saw and recognized the body lying 20
on the ground where Douglas had left it. 'Ah! Sir Walter
Blunt — there's "honour" for you!'

The Prince of Wales came up and rebuked the knight
for standing idle in the middle of the battle.

'Oh, Hal, let me rest for a moment. I've done such 25
deeds! I've killed Percy.'

'Percy's still alive,' Harry informed him, 'and we have
many deaths to revenge. We must not waste any more
time. Lend me your sword.'

'Not if Percy's still alive!' Falstaff kept his sword and 30
instead handed the prince a bottle of wine — which
Harry threw angrily back at him. 'I don't like such
honour as Sir Walter Blunt has,' muttered Falstaff. 'I'd
rather have life!'

The death of Hotspur

The battle continued all day. The two princes, Harry and young John of Lancaster, fought bravely. Douglas finally found the king, and Harry returned just in time
5 to save his father's life. Then Hotspur appeared in front of Harry, and challenged him to fight.

The Prince of Wales did not hesitate. 'You're not going to share glory with me any more, Percy!' he declared. 'England's not big enough to hold Harry Percy
10 and the Prince of Wales!'

'Then it's time for one of us to die!' shouted Hotspur.

The two men fought long and hard, watched by Falstaff — who was attacked by Douglas at just the moment Harry finally ran his sword through Hotspur.
15 Falstaff and Hotspur both fell to the ground.

'Oh, Harry, you have robbed me of my youth,' whispered Hotspur as he died. 'The glory is all yours now, and this wounds me more than your sword.'

Harry looked down in sadness. 'God be with you,
20 brave Percy, great heart!' he declared. 'While you lived, a kingdom was too small for you, and now this little bit of earth is large enough.' He covered Hotspur's face and then noticed Falstaff lying on the ground nearby.

'What, old friend, couldn't your huge body keep a
25 little life in it? Poor Jack, goodbye. I'll bury you later. Until then, lie in blood by noble Percy.'

Falstaff rises from the dead

The prince went back into the battle — and Falstaff stood up.
30 'Bury me? I'll not be buried today! But it was certainly time to pretend: that hot Scot would have killed me! Well, it's better to be careful than brave. God, but I'm

afraid of this fiery Percy, even if he is dead. And what
if he's pretending too, and rises from the dead like me?
Nobody's looking. I'll make sure he's dead and swear
that it was I who killed him.'

Falstaff pulled out his dagger and gave the lifeless   5
Hotspur a new wound in his leg. Then he picked up
the body and was starting to carry it away
as Harry returned with his brother.
The two princes looked at Falstaff,
astonished.

'But didn't you tell me that
this fat man was dead?'
John asked Harry.

'I did! I saw him
myself on the ground,
not breathing!' exclaimed Harry.

Falstaff, seeing them approach, threw Hotspur's body
down in front of them. 'Well, there's Percy!' he declared.
'If your father cares to give me honours, that's fine. If
not, let him kill the next Percy himself. But I expect to   20
be made an earl, I assure you.'

Even Harry could hardly believe what he heard. 'I
killed Percy myself,' he protested, 'and saw you dead!'

'All lies!' Falstaff said cheerfully. 'I was down and out
of breath, Hal, I admit. But then Percy and I both rose   25
and fought for a whole hour!'

'This is the strangest story I ever heard,' said Prince
John.

'This is the strangest man, brother John!' replied
Harry. Then he whispered in the knight's ear, 'If your

lie will help you, I'll support it.' Then the trumpets sounded across the battlefield. 'Victory!' Harry cried joyfully. 'The rebels have been defeated!'

He and his brother ran to find the king and Falstaff
5 slowly followed, carrying Hotspur's body. 'If I'm made an earl,' he promised, 'I shall repent and live a good life, as a nobleman should.'

Victory for King Henry

The trumpets sounded again and the king arrived with
10 his nobles, to see Worcester and Vernon led forward as prisoners. Henry now knew that they had not told Hotspur about his offer of a pardon, and his voice as he rebuked Worcester was bitter. 'The Earl of Stafford and many other good men would still be alive,' he
15 cried, 'if you had carried the truth between our armies like a Christian!'

Worcester offered no excuse and the king sent him and Vernon away to their deaths. The Earl of Douglas was also a prisoner but, for his courage, he was at
20 Harry's request allowed to return to Scotland without a ransom.

However, there was still rebellion in the land and the king had to deal with it without delay. 'You, son John and Westmoreland, go east to York to meet
25 Northumberland and Archbishop Scroop, who are gathering armies to fight against us,' he ordered. 'Harry, you and I will go west to Wales, to fight Glendower and the Earl of March.'

The trumpets sounded again over the battlefield as
30 Henry the Fourth declared to all his men:

'Rebellion in this land will go away,
If we fight on as we have fought today!'

HENRY THE FOURTH, PART II: FALSTAFF'S LIES

News reaches Northumberland

At the Battle of Shrewsbury, King Henry the Fourth had defeated the rebels led by the Earl of Worcester and his nephew Harry Percy. Percy's father, the old Earl of Northumberland, had remained at his castle. Now, one of his men brought him news from the battlefield. 5

'Morton!' Northumberland welcomed the messenger eagerly. 'You've come from Shrewsbury?'

'I've run from Shrewsbury, my lord,' Morton replied.

'You tremble and look pale!' Northumberland looked 10 at him in fear. 'How are my son and brother, and noble Douglas?'

Morton hesitated, not wanting to announce the dreadful news. 'Douglas and your brother Worcester are still alive. But your son —'

'He's dead! I can read it in your face!' cried the earl.

'It's true,' Morton admitted. He himself had seen the king's son Harry, the Prince of Wales, kill Harry Percy. After that, everything was soon over, he said. When the rebel soldiers learned that Percy, the great Hotspur, was
5 dead, they fled. Worcester was taken prisoner, and then the brave Douglas. 'So the king won the battle,' Morton finished, 'and now he's sending an army against you, led by young Prince John of Lancaster and the Earl of Westmoreland.'

10 The news of his son's death made Northumberland almost mad with grief. But his men urged him not to give up. Hotspur had had poor soldiers: the word 'rebellion' had frightened them, they said. But now Richard Scroop, the Archbishop of York, had an army
15 and was supporting them. The situation had changed. 'He turns rebellion into a religion,' Morton declared, 'claiming that God supports his cause, that England is suffering under Henry Bolingbroke and that the murder of King Richard the Second must be revenged ...'

20 Northumberland was calmer now. 'Yes, revenge must be taken,' he said.

The earl changes his mind

In his palace at York, Archbishop Scroop met Lord Mowbray and Lord Hastings, and they decided to
25 continue the rebellion. They hated Henry for deposing Richard, and they had 25,000 men — as many as the king. But they needed the support of the powerful Earl of Northumberland.

Old Northumberland decided to give them that
30 support. Then, just as he had done before the Battle of Shrewsbury, he changed his mind.

His wife and daughter-in-law, still in tears over Hotspur's death, begged him not to go to the wars.

'I must,' Northumberland said. 'It is a matter of honour.'

'Honour?' cried Lady Percy, Hotspur's widow. 'You broke your promise to go to Shrewsbury. Your own Percy, my darling Harry, looked for you, waited for you there. Two honours were lost then, yours and your son's. You left him, England's hero, alone on the battlefield! Is your honour more important now than it was then? The archbishop has enough support. If my dear Harry had had half as much, he might still be alive and Harry, Prince of Wales, dead instead.'

Nonetheless, Northumberland said that he must go and face the danger before it was too late.

Lady Northumberland, his wife, begged him to flee to Scotland until the new rebellion showed signs of success. Lady Percy begged him not to join the rebels yet. 'Don't go now, at the beginning,' she urged. 'That's what your son did. That's how I became a widow.'

Northumberland looked from one of them to the other, but he could not decide. He wanted to join the archbishop and yet —

'I'll go to Scotland,' he agreed suddenly, 'until the time is right.'

Falstaff meets the Lord Chief Justice

Sir John Falstaff, the Prince of Wales's tavern companion, returned to London after the Battle of Shrewsbury. But the king had ordered him to join the expedition being led by Prince John and Westmoreland against the Archbishop of York and the Earl of Northumberland.

Sir John was preparing to depart when, in the street, he saw the Lord Chief Justice. This Lord Chief Justice was a bold man. He had once sent the Prince of Wales to prison for hitting him, and Falstaff did not want to meet him. So he hurried on.

'That's the man who was questioned about the Gad's Hill robbery!' exclaimed the Chief Justice. 'Sir John
5 Falstaff!' he called.

'Say that I'm deaf,' Falstaff ordered his page, a boy servant given to him by Prince Harry.

'My master is deaf,' announced the page.

'I'm sure he is — to anything good!' said the Chief
10 Justice. 'Sir John Falstaff, I want to speak to you!'

Falstaff gave in. 'Oh, good day, my Lord Chief Justice! I'm glad to see you. Are you quite well, my lord?'

'Sir John, I ordered you to come and see me before you went to Shrewsbury.'

15 'I hear that His Majesty has left Wales,' Falstaff said brightly. (The king had gone into Wales with Harry after the battle, to fight the rebels Owen Glendower and Edmund Mortimer.)

'I'm not talking about His Majesty. You did not come
20 to see me.'

'And I hear His Majesty is not well —'

'Listen to me, Sir John! I wanted to see you about a serious matter, a matter involving the punishment of hanging.'

25 'I could not come because I was on military service,' said Falstaff.

'Well, you're lucky,' said the Chief Justice. 'Your day's service at Shrewsbury means your night's action at Gad's Hill can be pardoned. But you've been a bad
30 influence on the prince and I'm warning you —'

'If you're thinking of that time when the prince hit you,' said Falstaff, 'I've rebuked him for it and the young lion repents ...'

The Chief Justice sighed. 'May God send the prince
35 a better companion!'

'God send the companion a better prince!' replied Falstaff.

'I hear that the king has separated you and Prince Harry, and that you're going to York with his brother John to fight the archbishop.'   5

Now Falstaff sighed. 'Yes,' he said, 'every time there is a dangerous expedition, England sends me on it. I wish my name did not put fear into the enemy but, heigh-ho, that's how it is!'

The Chief Justice gave up. 'Well, be honest, and God   10
bless your expedition!'

The knight sensed victory. 'Will you lend me a thousand pounds?' he asked.

'Not a penny!' exclaimed the Lord Chief Justice, and walked on.   15

Falstaff cursed him, then asked the page how much money he had in his purse.

'Two shillings and sixpence,' the boy informed him.

'I can't cure this disease of the purse, and borrowing just makes it worse!' declared the knight. 'Go, boy, take   20
this letter to Prince Harry, and these letters to Prince John and the Earl of Westmoreland.'

'Arrest that man!'

Falstaff owed money to Mistress Quickly, hostess of the tavern in Eastcheap. He had gone off to the wars   25
without paying her, so now she stood out in the street with an officer of the law, waiting for Falstaff to walk by.

'I'm ruined!' Mistress Quickly told the sergeant. 'Sixty pounds is too much for a poor woman to be owed.   30
The knight's given me one excuse after another for not paying. There's no honesty in him...' She saw Falstaff coming along the street with his page and the red-nosed

Bardolph, and she grew very excited. 'There he is! Seize him, Master Sergeant, seize him!'

The officer stepped forward. 'Sir John Falstaff,' he announced, 'I arrest you for owing money to Mistress Quickly.'

'Arrest Sir John Falstaff? Away, you knave!' Falstaff roared. 'Bardolph, draw your sword! Cut off his head! Knock the woman down!'

'Murder!' screamed Mistress Quickly.

'Help!' shouted the sergeant.

'Keep them away, Bardolph,' ordered Falstaff.

The page danced merrily around Mistress Quickly. 'Go away, old woman, or I'll give you something to scream about!'

Suddenly, the Lord Chief Justice appeared with his men. 'Keep the peace here!' he ordered. Then he saw Falstaff. 'Fighting in the street, Sir John?' he demanded angrily. 'You should be on your way to York. What's the matter?'

Mistress Quickly was in tears. 'Oh, my most noble lord, I'm a poor widow of Eastcheap, and he,' she cried, pointing at Falstaff, 'owes me money!'

Falstaff asked what he owed her altogether.

'Altogether?' Altogether, he owed her sixty pounds and he had also promised to marry her, she claimed. 'You swore to me at Whitsun, that day at the tavern when the prince hit you in an argument about his father — you swore then, when I was washing your wound, that you would make me your lady-wife! And then you kissed me and asked me to fetch you thirty shillings …'

Falstaff let Mistress Quickly finish, then informed the Lord Chief Justice that she was a mad woman.

'Sir John, how you turn the truth upside-down!' exclaimed the Chief Justice, and ordered Falstaff to pay his debt.

But Falstaff did not give in so easily. As the Chief Justice turned away to receive a messenger from the court, the knight took the hostess to one side. 'I'll pay you back,' he promised her sweetly, 'on my honour as a gentleman! Of course I will! Just give me another ten pounds first. Come, if you didn't get so cross sometimes, you'd be one of the best women in England! Wash your face now and send this sergeant away. Come, don't be cross …'

And Mistress Quickly was persuaded yet again. She even asked the knight to supper, and offered to ask his friend, Doll Tearsheet, as well.

'No more words,' said Falstaff. 'Let's have her — and that ten pounds.'

Falstaff's letter to Harry

The king and his eldest son Prince Harry, the Prince of Wales, had now returned from Wales to England, but the king was ill and Harry was sad because of it.

'I tell you,' he said to his tavern friend Ned Poins, 'my heart bleeds that my father is so sick.'

'Your heart bleeds for your father!' exclaimed Poins, surprised. 'You can't mean it, after all this time when you've been so close to Falstaff!'

'And to you,' said Harry quietly, but Poins did not notice.

Bardolph and the page arrived, bringing Falstaff's letter to the prince, and Poins looked at Bardolph's ever-red face. 'What, still blushing, you fool?'

'His eyes are like two holes cut in a red skirt!' laughed the little page, and the prince and Poins, pleased with his joke, threw him coins.

Then Harry read out Falstaff's letter:

'Sir John Falstaff, Knight, to the son of the king nearest his father, Harry, Prince of Wales: I greet you! I think well of you! I am going away! Be careful of Poins. Repent when you have time. Goodbye.

Yours, Jack Falstaff to my friends, John to my family and Sir John to all Europe.'

Harry and Poins looked at each other, astonished. Then the prince asked, 'Is Falstaff still in London?'

'Yes,' said Bardolph. 'He is going to have supper tonight at the tavern, with old Mistress Quickly and Doll Tearsheet.'

'Who's Doll Tearsheet?' asked Harry, and an idea came to him. 'Let's disguise ourselves as servants and watch him, Ned!'

'I'm your shadow, I'll follow you,' Poins said.

'You boy, and Bardolph,' ordered the prince, 'don't tell your master that I'm back in town yet. Here's money for your silence.'

'I have no tongue, sir,' Bardolph smiled.

'And I'll hold mine, sir,' laughed the page.

HENRY THE FOURTH, PART II: A TROUBLED KING

Doll and Pistol come to the tavern

It was a busy evening at the tavern. Doll Tearsheet had drunk plenty of wine and, her face bright red, she joked and argued noisily with Falstaff. 'Come, I'll be friends with you, Jack,' she declared at last. 'You're going off   5
to the wars and who knows if I'll ever see you again?'
She looked into his eyes.

Bardolph entered to say that Pistol was below, wanting to speak to her.

'Hang the rogue!' shouted Doll. 'Don't let him come   10
up. He's got the dirtiest mouth in England!'

'If he's rude, don't let him in,' said Mistress Quickly. 'I must protect my good name: the sergeant said so. I won't have him in here if he is rude. Shut the door, I pray you.'   15

But Falstaff wanted to see him, and so Pistol came roaring up the stairs with Bardolph and the page, demanding to see Doll — and Doll told him to go away. 'You're a rogue and a thief,' she said, 'and anyway I am with Falstaff.'   20

'What!' Pistol roared even more loudly and he threatened to tear the clothes from her body.

Falstaff told him to leave.

'I'll see her damned first! To hell, say I! Down! Down! Revenge!' Pistol drew his sword.   25

Mistress Quickly, nervous for her 'good name', begged him to be quiet. Then, when he continued to shout and roar, Doll told her companions to throw him down the stairs.

'Throw me downstairs? What! Shall we shed blood? Then I'll kill you!' declared Pistol, waving his sword around.

'Murder!' screamed Mistress Quickly for the second time that day, as Falstaff took up his own sword and advanced.

'How you sweat, poor ape! Come, let me wipe your face,' Doll said to the knight as Pistol disappeared quickly down the stairs. 'Ah, rogue, I love you! You're as brave as the great hero, Hector of Troy, and worth five of Agamemnon!' she declared, sitting on his knee. 'But when are you going to stop fighting and get that old body ready for heaven?'

The prince in disguise

Some musicians began to play. Disguised as servants, the prince and Poins entered the room as Doll put her arms around Falstaff and went on talking.

'What is the prince like?' she asked.

'Very shallow,' declared Falstaff.

'And Poins? What is he like?'

'Stupid,' he said. 'The pair have able bodies but weak minds.'

'I could cut off his ears for this!' muttered Harry.

'Let's beat him in front of the woman,' Poins whispered back.

'Kiss me, Doll,' Falstaff said then, and Doll kissed him gladly. 'But I am old, I am old,' said the knight, sighing heavily.

'I love you better than I love any of the boys,' Doll comforted him.

'I'll buy you a dress when I receive some money!' Falstaff smiled around the room. 'Come, let's have a merry song! And then let's go to bed!'

'Get me some more wine to go with our song,' Doll said, looking round for the servants.

Falstaff called for more wine — and Harry and Poins stepped forward to serve him. 'Why, you ball of sin, what a life you lead!' declared Harry.

Mistress Quickly clapped her hands with delight at the sight of the prince. 'God bless your sweet face! Welcome back to London!'

'The king's mad son! I swear by this wicked woman,' exclaimed Falstaff, laying a hand on Doll's head, 'you are welcome.'

Poins urged Harry to take his revenge quickly, before Falstaff turned everything into a joke. So Harry protested that the knight had spoken of him very rudely to his lady-friend.

'Did you hear me?' asked Falstaff.

'Yes,' said Harry. 'And you knew me all the time — just like at Gad's Hill — and you did it purposely, to annoy me?'

'No', Falstaff admitted, 'I did not know that you were there. But I meant no harm to you or Ned, Hal, on my honour.'

'No harm!' repeated Poins.

'No harm in the world, Ned.' Falstaff turned to the prince, his excuse ready. 'I spoke badly of you to these wicked people,' (he waved at Doll and the others) 'because I didn't want them to fall in love with you. That was the reason!'

'So, to save yourself, you call this lady wicked?' cried Harry. 'And your hostess and the boy and honest Bardolph, all wicked?'

One of their friends knocked at the tavern door with news from the king's court. The king was now at the Palace of Westminster, he announced, and messengers had arrived from the north.

Harry left immediately with Poins, blaming himself for his absence from the court. 'Give me my sword and cloak. Falstaff, good night,' was all he said.

Then there was more knocking. Twelve army captains were at the door, waiting for Falstaff to go to the court also.

'Pay the musicians, boy,' Falstaff ordered his page. 'You see, my good women, how men of action are in demand… Goodbye, goodbye!' he called, as he went off with Bardolph and the boy.

'My heart will burst,' cried Doll. 'Sweet Jack, take care!'

'Goodbye, dear Sir John!' cried Mistress Quickly.

'Mistress Tearsheet!' Bardolph had returned. 'Please come to my master.'

Doll, in tears, ran after him.

Memories

King Henry had returned to London but he was still sick, in mind as well as body. He could not forget that he had deposed his cousin, King Richard the Second. He could not sleep because of it. Sleep came more easily to his poorest subjects than to him, the king. After midnight, still not able to sleep, he called in the Earl of Warwick — and Warwick, to comfort him, said that Prince John's army would quickly defeat the rebel Earl of Northumberland.

Northumberland! The name brought back disturbing
memories to Henry. Ten years ago, King Richard and
Northumberland had been great friends. Then, in 1399,
this same Northumberland had become his, Henry
Bolingbroke's, closest companion.   5

'Do you remember, Warwick?' asked the troubled
king. 'Richard called Northumberland "the ladder by
which my cousin Bolingbroke climbs to my throne".
Yet, God knows, I did not mean to … ' The king brought
his thoughts back to the present rebellion. 'They say   10
that Northumberland and the Archbishop of York have
50,000 men,' he said.

Warwick assured him that the rebels had only half
that number. There was good news, too: Glendower,
the rebel Welshman, was dead. The earl begged the   15
king to go to bed and rest, and the king finally agreed.
As soon as these wars were over, he said, they would
go to the Holy Land.

Meanwhile, Captain Sir John Falstaff left London, to
go north, fighting for the king against the rebels. But   20
he had to recruit his own company of foot-soldiers, so
on the way up he stopped at the estate of an old friend,
Justice Shallow. There he examined several possible
recruits, chose the poorest, and collected three pounds
offered by each of the others to avoid military service.   25

Falstaff then had dinner with Shallow and heard his
endless stories about their time together in London as
young men.

'Ah, the times you and I have had together!' declared
Shallow.   30

'We've heard the bells at midnight, Master Shallow,'
Falstaff sighed.

Shallow now had money, land and cattle. Falstaff had
nothing, and he did not like it. So he agreed to visit
Shallow again on his way home from the wars.   35

'Lord bless you, Sir John!' cried Shallow as Falstaff departed with his recruits. 'Come here on your return and we'll talk about old times again. Then perhaps I'll come with you to court.'

5 'Yes,' said Falstaff. 'I'll come back,' he promised himself, 'and get some money out of this Justice Shallow. He does nothing except tell tales of his time as a law student — and every third word's a lie! He talks about the king's father, John of Gaunt, as if they'd

10 been close friends and, I swear, he only ever saw him once. Lord, how old men do lie!'

In Gaultree Forest

Led by its general, Prince John, the king's army was now advancing on the rebels, who had gathered in

15 Gaultree Forest to the north of York city. Both sides had about 25,000 men, but the Earl of Northumberland had gone to Scotland instead of joining the rebellion. Archbishop Scroop had just given this bad news to Mowbray and Hastings when the Earl of Westmoreland

20 rode into their camp.

'Why have you raised an army against the king? You should be a man of peace, Your Grace,' Westmoreland said to the archbishop. 'Why do you turn your pen into a sword and the word of God into a trumpet of war?'

25 'Since the death of King Richard, the whole kingdom has been sick, and I am trying to bring it back to health,' Scroop replied. 'King Henry has always refused to meet me to discuss the country's troubles.'

'That is not true,' claimed Westmoreland.

30 'Nonetheless, to avoid war, my general, Prince John, is willing to see the rebels and discuss their complaints.'

Mowbray was suspicious, but Hastings and the archbishop agreed to a meeting. The king was tired of

civil war, they assured Mowbray. If they made peace
with his son now, that peace would be 'as strong as a
mountain'. So they gave Westmoreland a list of their
complaints, and waited.

Prince John then called the rebel lords to a meeting-   5
place in the forest, between their two armies. His
father's court had made mistakes, he admitted. He,
John, had now read and understood the rebels'
complaints, and he would settle them quickly.

'I promise you, I shall,' the prince declared. 'So send   10
your men home, as we shall, too. And, in front of both
our armies, let us drink together here as friends. Good
health to you, my Lord of York!' he said to the
archbishop.

'Good health to you, Lord Mowbray!' declared   15
Westmoreland.

'I may need your good wishes,' muttered Mowbray.

Hastings sent a captain to pay his soldiers and tell
them to go home, and Prince John ordered
Westmoreland to do the same. But as soon as Hastings   20
reported that the rebel army had departed in all
directions, Westmoreland stepped in front of him.

'You give us good news, my Lord Hastings,'
he declared. 'I now arrest you as a traitor...
And you, my Lord Archbishop...
And you, Lord Mowbray...
I arrest you all.'

Falstaff is lucky

The three lords were taken prisoner and the king's men
chased the departing rebel soldiers, Falstaff finally
arrived in the forest with Bardolph, his page and his
5 poor company of recruits. He was lucky. A rebel called
Sir John Colevile knelt in front of him and offered him
his sword just as the fighting stopped.

Prince John appeared with the Earl of Westmoreland,
telling him to call back all their men. 'Falstaff!' he
10 exclaimed angrily when he saw the knight. 'Where have
you been all this time? One day, I swear, you'll be
hanged for these delaying tricks of yours!'

Falstaff looked hurt. 'My lord! I've come here as fast
as my poor old body could bring me. And, tired though
15 I am, I've just made this bold knight my prisoner.'

Prince John sighed. 'Send Colevile to his death with
the other rebels,' he told Westmoreland. 'The king, my
father, is very sick. Take our good news to the court to
comfort him, and I'll follow as fast as I can.'

20 Falstaff asked the prince to speak well of him when
he returned to the court.

'I'll speak better of you than you deserve,' John
replied without a smile.

Falstaff watched the prince as he departed. 'I cannot
25 make that boy laugh!' he grumbled. 'But that's because
he drinks no wine. A good wine goes straight to the
brain, making it quick and fiery. It lights the face and
warms the blood, giving the heart courage. That's why
Prince Harry is brave: he's added wine to the cold blood
30 he got from his father... Eh, my red-nosed Bardolph?'

Bardolph reported that the king's soldiers had now
gone home.

'Good,' said Falstaff. 'Then we'll return to Master
Shallow's.'

HENRY THE FOURTH, PART II: THE KING DIES

The king's last illness

In the Jerusalem Hall of the Palace of Westminster, King Henry lay weak and ill, talking to the Earl of Warwick. As soon as the present rebellion was defeated and he himself was a little stronger, the king said, he would 5 lead the promised expedition to the Holy Land.

Two of Henry's four sons were standing nearby, and he asked them where their eldest brother was.

Henry's youngest son, Humphrey of Gloucester, hesitated. 'I think he's gone to hunt in Windsor Forest, 10 my lord.'

'Then why aren't you with him, Thomas?' the king asked the other prince.

Thomas of Clarence looked away. 'Harry's not at Windsor today,' he said. 'He's here in London.' 15

'Who's with him?' demanded his father.

'Poins,' Thomas replied slowly, 'and some of his usual companions.'

The king held his head in grief and despair, thinking beyond his own death to Harry's reign. 'Imagine when 20 he's your king!' he cried out. 'When he's in power, with nobody to control him. On his way to ruin —'

'My lord, you're wrong about him!' Warwick tried to comfort the king, assuring him that, when the time came, the Prince of Wales would dismiss his present 25 companions.

The Earl of Westmoreland suddenly entered the hall. 'Good health to Your Majesty and good news from your son, Prince John of Lancaster!' The Earl had arrived back

in London and now came to announce the victory at
York, and another great victory over the Earl of
Northumberland and the Scots.

'Oh, Westmoreland, you bring good news indeed!'
5 exclaimed the king — and fainted, falling to the ground.

Gently, the two princes lifted their father and carried
him to a bed in the next room. Opening his eyes for a
moment, the king told them to place his royal crown
beside him on the pillow. Then he lay back.

10 'Less noise! Less noise there!' ordered Warwick as
Harry marched in, looking for his brother Thomas, and
saw his father lying very still on the bed.

'What's the matter?' Harry demanded.

Humphrey told his brother that the king was very ill.

15 'Perhaps he's sick with joy at the good news!'
declared Harry.

'Not so much noise, my lords!' urged Warwick again.
'Your father wants to sleep.'

'Let's go back into the hall,' whispered Thomas.

20 Suddenly Harry realized that their father was dying.
'I'll sit here by the king,' he told his brothers quietly.

The golden crown

Harry sat by the bed, looking at his father and at the
golden crown that had destroyed him. The king did not
25 seem to move or breathe.

Sadly, Harry lifted the crown from the pillow and as
Henry's eldest son, Prince of Wales, heir to the throne
of England, he put it on his own head. 'No one will
ever take this crown from me,' he swore. 'I shall leave
30 it to my heirs as it is now left to me.' Still wearing the
crown, he went out of the room by another door.

Some minutes passed. Then the king called out in a
weak voice, 'Warwick! Gloucester! Clarence!'

They hurried in from the hall, surprised to find him alone. 'We left Harry my brother here,' said Thomas of Clarence. 'He promised to sit and watch by you.'

'The Prince of Wales? Where is he?' asked the king eagerly.

'He hasn't come past us,' replied Humphrey of Gloucester.

'And where is my crown?' the king demanded. 'Is Harry in such a hurry for it that he imagines me dead already?' He told Warwick to find the prince and send him in again. 'See, my sons, what things men become when they want gold!' His voice was bitter.

Then Harry ran back into the room. 'My lord, I never expected to hear you speak again!'

The king sent everyone else away. 'You wanted me dead, Harry!' he accused his son. 'You foolish youth! Couldn't you wait another hour for the throne? Then go: dig my grave yourself and ring the merry bells to say that you are crowned! Harry the Fifth is crowned! Away, good sense! Let every idle ape gather at the English court...! Oh, my poor kingdom, already sick with civil war, what will happen to you now?'

With tears running down his face, Harry knelt beside his father, holding out the crown and begging to be forgiven.

'Here is your crown, my most royal lord, long may it still be yours!' he cried. 'As God's my witness, my heart turned cold when I came in and thought you were dead. "This crown has murdered my father," I said, and
5 I swear I put it on only to accuse it. If I showed any joy, let me never be crowned, let the world never see how I meant to change!'

The king held out his hands, believing and trusting in his son at last. 'Come here, Harry,' he said. 'Sit by
10 my bed and listen to the last advice I'll ever give.'

Then Henry warned his heir of the dangers he would face during his reign. Harry's claim to the throne was much stronger than his, he said. Nonetheless, many of the great lords of the land had only recently been the
15 king's enemies and might still want a different man to be king.

'That is why,' the king admitted, 'to keep these same lords busy, I wanted to lead an expedition to the Holy Land. And that is why you, my Harry, should start some
20 foreign quarrels, to prevent rebellion at home...' His voice became weaker, and he stopped.

John of Lancaster, just back from the north, entered in time to greet his father. Then Henry, having seen all his sons, asked the faithful Warwick to carry him back
25 into the Jerusalem Hall to die. He said that it would remind him of the Holy Land.

Harry, King of England

And so, at the Palace of Westminster, in the year 1413, Henry Bolingbroke died and Harry, his eldest son,
30 became Henry the Fifth, King of England.

This was bad news for the Lord Chief Justice, who had once sent Harry to prison for hitting him, and the lords at the palace immediately warned him.

'The young king has no love for you,' claimed the Earl of Warwick.

'You've lost a friend indeed!' declared Humphrey of Gloucester.

'You're in more danger than any of us,' said John of Lancaster.

'You'll have to speak well of Sir John Falstaff now!' exclaimed Thomas of Clarence.

The Lord Chief Justice shook his head. He had always acted with honour, he said. He would not change or beg for pardon.

Trumpets sounded through the palace and the new king approached. He stopped when he saw the princes and looked at them closely. 'Brothers, I see you mix your sadness with some fear,' he declared. 'Yet, by heaven, I'll be your father and your brother too. One Henry's dead, and we'll shed tears for him. But another Henry lives who'll turn those tears to joy ...'

The Lord Chief Justice moved forward. 'God save Your Majesty!' he said.

'Ah!' said King Henry. 'The man who sent me to prison!'

Quietly, the Chief Justice defended his action. He was representing the king's law in the king's court, at the time when Harry had hit him. Would the new king allow a son of his to do such a thing? Or would he expect his Lord Chief Justice to protect the majesty and power of the law and punish that son as he had punished Harry?

'Imagine the case with yourself as king and father,' he ordered, 'and tell me what I did that was wrong.'

The young king listened in silence. Then he held out his hand. 'What you did was right,' he said. 'I want you to continue as Lord Chief Justice, acting in the same bold, honest way against others as you did against me.'

He had buried his own wild ways in his father's grave, he promised, and he would now prove it to the world. 'As soon as I've been crowned, I'll appoint the best advisers in the land, for war or peace. And you, my Lord Chief Justice, shall help me.'

Falstaff hears the good news

Sir John Falstaff, not knowing what had happened at Westminster, was still at Justice Shallow's estate in the country, with Bardolph and the little page.

Shallow, wanting a friend at court, wanted Falstaff to stay; and Falstaff, wanting to borrow some money from Shallow, did not want to leave. They had just had supper and were singing and drinking merrily together out of doors. 'Mmm, you've got a good place here, and rich!' Sir John informed old Shallow.

'No, no, very poor, but the air's good… Some wine for Master Bardolph!' Shallow ordered a servant. 'Be merry, my little soldier,' he was saying kindly to the page, when the servant ran back to say that Pistol had arrived with news from the court.

Pistol was already close behind. 'Sweet knight,' he announced to Falstaff, bending low, 'you are now one of the greatest men in the kingdom! Your friend Pistol has ridden with all speed from London to bring you the happy news! I tell of lucky joys, of golden times…'

'If you have news from the court, give it straight!' ordered Shallow. 'By my authority under the king —'

'Under which king?' demanded Pistol. 'Speak or die!'

'Why, King Henry the Fourth,' replied Shallow.

'Then I care nothing for your authority,' Pistol declared. 'Henry the Fifth's the man now!'

'What? Is the old king dead?' Falstaff began to smile, and his smile grew until it stretched right across his face.

'Away, Bardolph, fetch my horse!' he shouted joyfully. 'Pistol, I'll load you with honours for this! Master Shallow, ask for any position in the land: it's yours! Put on your boots, my Lord Shallow. We'll ride all night, the young king will need me. Blessed are those that have been my friends — and down with the Lord Chief Justice!'

'God save my Hal!'

Falstaff and his followers rode back into London on the day that Harry was crowned King of England. They stood outside Westminster Abbey, waiting for the ceremony to finish, and Falstaff gave them their orders.

'Stand here by me, Master Shallow, and I'll make the king give you a good position. You'll see how he smiles at me. You, Pistol, stand here behind me. Bardolph, boy ...'

The knight had managed to borrow a thousand pounds from Justice Shallow and wished he had had time to buy new clothes. 'But it doesn't matter, eh, Shallow? These poor clothes show how I rode day and night, how I stand here, sweating with travel, thinking of nothing but seeing him, forgetting everything else —'

Shouts and the sound of trumpets came from within the great church as the crown was placed on the king's head. Then Henry the Fifth appeared to his subjects outside, surrounded by his court.

'God save Your Grace, King Hal, my Hal!' Falstaff shouted as the royal procession approached.

The king turned to the Lord Chief Justice and ordered him to speak to 'that foolish man'. But the knight pushed through the crowd, up to the king himself. 'God save you, my sweet boy!' he laughed.

King Henry looked at him, as though he was looking through him. 'I don't know you, old man,' he declared — and sent Falstaff away for ever from the court. 'Provide him with money. Help him if he mends his ways,' he ordered the Lord Chief Justice, 'but let him never come within ten miles of me again.'

The procession moved on, but Falstaff did not move. Suddenly he smiled. 'Don't be sad about this, Master
10   Shallow,' he said. 'The king has to behave like this in public. Yes, he'll send for me in private. I'm still the man who can make you great! Come with me to dinner, Master Shallow, Pistol. I shall be sent for soon at night, I promise you.'

15   But the knight was not sent for. Instead, the Lord Chief Justice sent him and his friends, including Doll Tearsheet, to prison.

Prince John of Lancaster smiled at last. His brother the king had done the right thing, he told the Chief
20   Justice. There were challenging times to come. Very soon, he felt certain, Henry would lead England to war against France.

8

HENRY THE FIFTH:
THE ENGLISH GO TO FRANCE

England's claim to France

Henry the Fifth, the new young King of England, did
as he had promised. He gave up the wild life he had
led as Prince Harry, and applied himself with all his
heart to the government of his country.   5

The people of England, now Henry's subjects, began
to love him, but Henry remembered his dying father's
advice to start some foreign quarrels to prevent
rebellion at home. He informed the French king that
the lands of several French dukes belonged to him,   10
Henry, through his great-grandfather Edward the Third.

An ambassador arrived at the palace with an answer
from France, but Henry first called in the Archbishop
of Canterbury. He wanted to know whether he, King
Henry the Fifth of England, had a strong claim to the   15
throne of France. His claim must be strong because so
many lives would be lost in a war between the two
kingdoms. He ordered the archbishop to advise him
very carefully.

The archbishop spoke for a long time, giving many   20
examples from his studies. Edward the Third's mother
was the daughter of a king of France. Henry's claim
therefore came through a woman. This did not matter,
as several French kings had come to the throne because
they had a female relation in the royal family.   25

'So it is a true claim?' Henry asked.

'Yes,' said the archbishop, wanting to please the king.

The lords around Henry's throne wanted to fight the
French.

'Then you shall fight!' cried the archbishop. 'The church will raise the money, Your Majesty, if you will raise the flag.'

The king listened carefully to his advisers. Then he called in the French ambassador.

The Dauphin's joke

The ambassador came into the throne-room and bowed low. He came from the Dauphin, eldest son and heir of the King of France. He asked the King of England whether he wanted the Dauphin's answer in plain or polite terms. Henry ordered him to speak plainly.

'Then here is the answer, Your Majesty. You have recently claimed several dukedoms of France. This is how my master, the prince, replies: "You still behave like a youth. France cannot be won like some game." The Dauphin therefore sends you this treasure as a present' — the ambassador waved forward a servant carrying a large box — 'and will not listen to your claims to any dukedoms.'

The king's uncle, the Duke of Exeter, was standing near the throne. 'What treasure is it, uncle?' Henry asked.

Exeter bent down and opened the box. 'Tennis balls, my lord!'

'Tennis balls!' King Henry looked at the French ambassador. 'We thank you for the Dauphin's present,' he said slowly. 'We will use it to play a game in France. With these balls we will hit the French king's crown right out of court! 5

'The Dauphin laughs at me for my wild youth. But tell the Dauphin, sir, that I am now a king, and when I am King of France also, I'll rise there like the sun and with so full a glory that I'll blind his eyes. Tell the pleasant prince that this joke of his will turn his tennis 10 balls to stones of war, make women into widows, and tear his castles down. Tell him,' Henry finished angrily, 'that I am coming now to take my revenge, and that thousands more will cry at his joke than laugh at it.'

He dismissed the ambassador, and the court went 15 wild with excitement. England would go to war with France! The Dauphin's joke with the tennis balls had decided it.

To France!

The excitement spread from the palace through the 20 whole land. All the youth of England wanted to go to France. From north to south in the year 1415, they ordered armour and bought horses, eager to follow King Henry across the sea to honour and glory.

Even the men of Eastcheap, in the poor part of 25 London, caught the excitement. Bardolph, who had been one of Harry's tavern companions when he was Prince of Wales, decided to go to France as a soldier. So did Pistol and their friend, Nim.

Pistol, thrown out by Doll Tearsheet, had married 30 Mistress Quickly, the tavern hostess, and that annoyed Nim, who had planned to marry her himself. But after a few quarrels, a few drawn swords, a few screams of

'Murder!' from Mistress Quickly, they decided to shake hands and go to France together.

'Still, I'll cut your throat one day, Pistol,' threatened Nim.

'You'll not get my wife, oh dog, oh snake, oh lying villain! I defy you!' roared Pistol, putting his hand on his sword again. 'Go down to the hospital and get yourself Doll Tearsheet instead!'

Sir John Falstaff's page ran out onto the street, interrupting them to beg Pistol and his wife to come to his master.

'Sir John is very sick and needs to go to bed.' The boy looked at Bardolph's red nose and laughed. 'Good Bardolph, you could put your face between his sheets and warm him!' He turned to Mistress Quickly. 'The knight is very ill,' he said.

'The king has killed his heart,' said the hostess sadly. 'Good husband, come in soon,' she called as she went indoors with the page.

'Come, be friends,' said Bardolph to Nim and Pistol. 'We're going to France together. We must fight the French and not each other.'

'Will you pay me the eight shillings that I won from you?' Nim asked Pistol.

'I will not pay!' declared Pistol.

'I will have the money!' said Nim.

Then Pistol drew his sword again, and Nim drew his — and Bardolph drew his, saying he would kill the first man who attacked. So Pistol immediately agreed to pay Nim. He could make money for them all in France, he boasted.

'Please come now, all of you!' Mistress Quickly ran out of the tavern.

'Poor Sir John is shaken with a dreadful fever.'

'The king has treated the knight badly,' said Nim.

'Nim, you are right,' allowed Pistol. 'The knight's heart is broken. Let us go in and comfort him.'

The death of Falstaff

By August of that year, England was ready to attack France and the king set out for the port of Southampton.

It was time for Pistol, Bardolph and Nim to leave too, but Sir John Falstaff had died and they felt lost.

'I'll come with you on the road,' said Mistress Quickly.

'No,' said Pistol, 'for my bold heart is sad. Bardolph, smile! Nim, be brave. Boy, take courage. Falstaff is dead and we must look after ourselves now.'

'I wish I was with him,' said Bardolph, 'whether he's in heaven or hell.'

'He's not in hell!' protested Mistress Quickly. 'He made a fine end and went away like any Christian child, just between twelve and one. When I saw him play with the sheets and smile at his fingers, I knew there was only one way it could finish. He spoke of green fields, and he cried out, "God, God, God". So I, to comfort him, told him he need not think of God, there was no need for him to trouble himself with any such thoughts yet. So he told me to put more clothes on his feet. I put my hand into the bed and felt them, and they were as cold as any stone. Then I felt to his knees, and so up and up, and all was as cold as any stone...'

'They say that he cried out against wine,' said Nim.

'Yes, he did,' agreed Mistress Quickly.

'And against women,' claimed Bardolph.

'No, he did not!'

'Yes, he did,' declared the page. 'He said they were devils. And he saw a black spot on Bardolph's nose and said it was a man burning in hell!'

'We must go,' Nim interrupted. 'The king is at Southampton.'

Pistol kissed his wife goodbye, and told her to look after the tavern and lend no money.

Then Lieutenant Bardolph kissed her. 'Goodbye, hostess.'

'I cannot kiss you now,' said Nim sadly. 'But goodbye.'

'Goodbye, goodbye,' replied Mistress Quickly, wiping away tears.

And so Falstaff's friends went off to war, taking his page with them.

'To France, my lads, to make some money!' roared Pistol.

Traitors in the camp

Most Englishmen supported Henry and his cause, but not all. His father Henry Bolingbroke had warned him that there might be trouble from those who had supported Richard the Second, and there was.

By the time the king reached Southampton, he knew that three of his nobles were traitors. His close friend Lord Scroop (nephew of the Archbishop of York who had rebelled against Bolingbroke), the Earl of Cambridge and Sir Thomas Grey had plotted with the French to murder him at the port.

Boldly, Henry decided to do nothing until they came to him there, to receive some letters of authority. Then he tricked them.

'Uncle,' he ordered the Duke of Exeter, 'release the man sent to prison yesterday for speaking against me. He had only drunk too much wine. I shall pardon him.'

'You show too much mercy, Your Majesty,' protested Scroop. 'The man should be punished, as an example to others.'

'Yes, punish him, my lord,' urged Cambridge.

'But shouldn't I show mercy?' asked the king.

'You'll be showing mercy, sir, if you allow him to live!' declared Grey.

'But if little faults can't be forgiven, what shall we do about great crimes?' asked Henry. 'No, I've decided. Let the man go free.'

He handed papers to Scroop, Cambridge and Grey, then turned to his uncle and said he would go on board ship that night. 'Why, gentlemen, what do you read that makes you look so pale?' he asked, turning back to the three nobles.

The papers they held were not the letters of authority they had expected, but documents accusing them of treason. The men fell to their knees, begging for mercy.

'You talk of mercy? How dare you, when you've just advised me to show none!' exclaimed the king. 'See these English devils!' he said to those around him. 'They sold themselves to France and swore to murder me here at Southampton. Cambridge, Grey and — worst of all — you, Lord Scroop, whom I trusted so completely.' His voice was bitter as he spoke to the man who had been his friend. 'You, who seemed so honourable, so God-fearing, so true... Your treason is the most terrible.'

He ordered Exeter to arrest the three men. He wanted no revenge for himself, he said, but they had put his kingdom in danger, and for that they must die. 'Take them away.'

By revealing this treason, God had shown that He was on England's side, Henry told his nobles. Everything would now go well with the expedition.

HENRY THE FIFTH:
ATTACKING THE FRENCH

A message for the Dauphin

The French knew that the English were coming and, at their court at Rouen on the River Seine, they discussed the need to defend themselves.

5   The French king, Charles the Sixth, said that the great dukes and the Dauphin should prepare their towns against attack.

    'Let's show no fear, though!' exclaimed the Dauphin. 'The English aren't serious. Their king is too idle and 10 too shallow.'

    'You're wrong, Prince Dauphin.' The High Constable of France, in command of the French army, thought the Dauphin foolish. 'The French ambassador found the English king sensible, well advised and determined.'

15   The French king agreed with his general. 'King Harry's strong,' he said, 'and you princes should be well prepared when you meet him in battle. It was his ancestors, Edward the Third and Edward the Black Prince of Wales, who shamed France at the Battle of 20 Crecy...'

    An English ambassador arrived, and the Dauphin urged his father on. 'Defy them, my lord! Then the coward dogs will stop the attack.'

    The Duke of Exeter was the ambassador and he 25 spoke as plainly to the King of France as the ambassador who brought the tennis balls had spoken to the King of England. 'My nephew tells you to give up your crown and kingdom, which properly belong to him.'

'And if I do not?' asked the French king.

'He'll come and take them by force. So he tells you to give them up now and show mercy on your poor subjects. That is his message to Your Majesty, and here is his claim.' The duke handed the king a document showing Henry's claim to the French throne through Edward the Third. 'I also have a message for the Dauphin.'

'What message? I want no peace with England,' said the Dauphin proudly. 'That's why I sent your idle young king the tennis balls.'

'He'll make your kingdom shake for it!' declared Exeter. 'Harry the king is very different from Harry the prince, I assure you. If your father doesn't accept his claim, he says, he'll make you pay for your little joke until France shakes with the noise of war.'

The king hesitated. He would give Exeter his answer the next day, he promised.

The siege of Harfleur

'Attack!'

Henry had sailed across the English Channel and landed with his army on the coast of Normandy. The French king did not give up his crown. He only offered Henry some minor dukedoms, plus his daughter, Katherine as his bride; he said that Henry could marry her. As he had sworn he would, Henry therefore went to war, first laying siege to the port of Harfleur, surrounding it and stopping supplies from reaching it.

'Once more, attack!' he cried, seizing England's flag of St George for all to see, urging his men forward to destroy the town walls. 'On, on, you noble English! Show these men how to fight! At the next charge, cry "God for Harry, England and St George!"'

Again the soldiers attacked. The air was loud with the clashing of the swords.

'On, on! To the walls, to the walls!' cried Bardolph in imitation.

5   Nim begged Bardolph to keep away from the fighting. 'It's too hot and dangerous!'

'I wish I was back in London at the tavern,' said the page.

'So do I,' said Pistol.

10   They stayed as far back as they could. Then a Welsh captain called Fluellen saw them and angrily drove the three men forward. 'Up to the walls, you dogs!'

The boy was left standing alone. 'They roar and boast, the three of them,' he muttered, 'but they're

15   thieves and cowards. And they expect me to steal too. I must leave the villains.'

The siege continued into September, under the command of the king's youngest brother Humphrey, Duke of Gloucester. The English tried to break down

20   the walls of Harfleur. They tried to climb them with ladders. They tried to pull them down from underneath. Still they could not get through.

But neither could the people of Harfleur get out. The Dauphin did not send the help they had begged for,

25   and at last they sounded a trumpet, requesting a pause in the fighting.

Henry advanced to the closed gates of the town. 'Either surrender now or defy us to do our worst!' he shouted. 'If the fighting starts again, you can expect no

30   mercy from us. So show some pity on your town, you men of Harfleur, while my soldiers are still under my control.'

The Governor of Harfleur came out onto the walls. He announced that his people could no longer defend

35   themselves and he ordered them to open the gates.

Henry, gentle now, told the Duke of Exeter to enter the town and show mercy to everyone in it. Winter was coming and many of his own soldiers were sick, he added. He would march them north, to the English base at Calais.

Decisions at Rouen

News of Henry's victory at Harfleur and his march towards Calais reached the French court at Rouen in October. The king and his lords were still discussing what to do.

'He is past the River Somme,' King Charles announced.

'My lord, if we don't fight him,' declared the Constable, 'France is lost!'

'My God!' exclaimed the Dauphin. 'Are we going to let barbarians conquer us?'

'If we don't challenge them,' announced the Duke of Bourbon, 'I'll sell my dukedom for a muddy farm on that wretched island of theirs.'

'Where do they get this iron will?' the Constable
5   asked. 'Their weather's dreadful, their beer's like water ...'

'Our women laugh at us,' complained the Dauphin. 'They say they'll give their bodies to the English youths, to supply France with better soldiers.'

10   'They say that we, the French, are good at only one thing, and that is running away!' said Bourbon.

King Charles hesitated no longer. 'Where is Montjoy the herald? Send him to defy the English king!' he cried. 'High Constable of France, you lords, great dukes,
15   princes and knights, go out and stop this Harry England. He thinks he can win the rest of France as easily as he won Harfleur. Stop him from reaching Calais and bring him here to me at Rouen as a prisoner.'

The Constable welcomed his king's decision. 'The
20   English king has so few men and his soldiers are so sick and hungry,' he told Charles, 'that when he sees our army, he'll offer us ransom money without a fight.'

'Then let Montjoy ask him what ransom he will give.' The king turned to his son. 'Prince Dauphin, you'll stay
25   here with us at Rouen.'

'Oh no, Your Majesty!' protested the Dauphin.

The Dauphin's sister, Princess Katherine, was also at the palace. She was more obedient than her brother, and she knew that her father had offered her as a bride
30   to the King of England. She decided to learn English.

'De hand, de fingers, de nails, de arm, and de elbow —' she recited proudly to her lady-in-waiting, Alice.

'De "elbow", madame,' Alice corrected her.

'De elbow,' Katherine repeated. 'De hand, de fingers,
35   de nails ...'

At the bridge

The English had crossed the Somme and then by 23rd October, under the Duke of Exeter, were fighting to cross the River Ternoise on their way north.

'Is the duke safe?' an English captain called Gower asked Captain Fluellen.

'Praise God, he is,' Fluellen replied. 'He keeps the bridge most bravely. One of his men is doing very good service … Here he is, Pistol.'

Pistol ran up to him, crying out that Exeter had ordered Bardolph to be hanged for stealing a holy picture from a church. 'Captain Fluellen, I beg you! The Duke of Exeter will listen to you. Speak for brave, unfortunate Bardolph. Let him not be hanged! Speak for his life and I will pay you …'

But Pistol had chosen the wrong man to ask. Military good behaviour was the most important thing in the world to Fluellen, and he refused to help. 'Soldiers must always behave correctly,' he said.

'Then be damned!' roared Pistol and ran off again.

Captain Gower told Fluellen that Pistol himself was a rogue and a thief. Then the king came up with his brother Gloucester, and asked how many men their uncle had lost at the bridge.

'None,' Fluellen told him, 'except one who is likely to be hanged for robbing a church. He's called Bardolph. Perhaps Your Majesty knows him. His face is fiery red …'

The king gave no sign that he knew Bardolph. 'I want all such thieves hanged,' he told Fluellen. 'Nothing must be stolen on our march through France.'

A trumpet sounded and Montjoy the herald appeared with his message from the King of France. 'My king defies you! He says, "Tell Harry England we could have challenged him at Harfleur, but we chose to wait. Tell him he will learn to repent his foolishness and admire our patience. Let him consider what ransom he will offer …"'

Henry listened carefully to the herald's words. 'Go back to Rouen, Montjoy,' he ordered, 'and tell your king I am not looking for a fight. My men are few and sick, and my only ransom is my own poor body. But I will march on to Calais. We don't want a battle, but we won't avoid one either. Tell your master that.'

Montjoy departed for the French court and Henry told his brother to lead the English army across the bridge. They would camp on the far side for the night and continue their march the next day, he said.

The French are confident

As King Charles had ordered, the Constable of France rode north with the great dukes to stop the English from reaching their base at Calais. The French were very confident of victory. They had many more men than Henry had brought across the Channel, and they had splendid horses.

They camped at a place called Agincourt and prepared to block the English advance. On 24th October, Henry camped within a mile of them, and they decided to challenge him the following day.

At midnight, the French lords were still talking together about the coming battle.

'Oh, how I wish it was day!' said the Constable. 'I have such good armour ...'

'Will morning never come?' sighed the Duke of Orleans. 'My horse is the best in Europe.'

'Such a long night!' grumbled the Duke of Bourbon. 'But I have the best horse in the world, and tomorrow he and I'll be riding over English faces together.' The duke went off to his tent.

'Bourbon looks forward to beating the English!' said Lord Rambures.

'But poor Harry England! He doesn't look forward to the dawn as we do. If the English had any sense in their heads, they'd run away,' said the Constable.

'But they haven't,' smiled Orleans. 'They wear such heavy armour that they cannot run away!'

'English men are like English dogs,' declared the Constable. 'Give them great meals of beef and they'll fight like devils.'

'Yes, but these English men have no more beef,' said Orleans.

'Then tomorrow we'll find that they want to eat, not fight!' the Constable told him. 'Come, it's time to get ready.'

'By ten o'clock,' Orleans boasted, 'we shall each have a hundred English prisoners!'

HENRY THE FIFTH: BEFORE THE BATTLE

Waiting for the dawn

No one was laughing or boasting in the English camp.

The two armies, English and French, were so close that they could see each other's camp fires, and hear
5 each other's horses and the sound of iron against iron as the knights' armour was made ready. But the English soldiers were tired and hungry and far from home, and they knew that the French army blocking their advance was much larger than theirs. They sat by their fires in
10 the moonlight and waited silently for the dawn.

At three in the morning, King Henry began to walk around the camp, visiting his men, from the highest to the lowest, encouraging them with brave words and a cheerful smile.
15 'Take courage, Gloucester!' he greeted one brother. 'Good morning, Clarence,' he greeted another. 'Our bad neighbour makes us rise early!'

An older man came out of his tent at the sound of the king's voice. 'Sir Thomas Erpingham, good morning
20 to you too!' Henry cried. 'A soft pillow would be better for that good white head of yours than the rough grass of France.'

He sent his brothers to greet all the nobles of the camp, then asked Erpingham to lend him his cloak.
25 'Shall I stay with you, Your Majesty?'

'No, my good old knight, go with my brothers. I want to be on my own now for a while.'

'God bless you, noble Harry!' Erpingham declared, and followed the two princes.

Soldiers of the king

'Who goes there?' Suddenly Pistol jumped in front of the king.

'A friend,' said Henry, disguised by Erpingham's cloak.

'Are you an officer, or an ordinary soldier?' demanded Pistol.

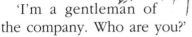

'I'm a gentleman of the company. Who are you?'

'As good a gentleman as the emperor,' came the boastful answer.

'Then you're better than the king?'

'Oh, the king has a brave heart, and I love the lad...! My name is Pistol. What is yours?'   15

'Harry King!' replied Henry the king. 'I'm from Wales.'

'Do you know Fluellen?'

'Yes, I know Fluellen.'

'Then tell him I'll knock him around the head if I see him!' roared Pistol and departed into the darkness.   20

Captain Gower approached, looking for Fluellen, and the king stood back out of sight.

'Captain Fluellen!'

Fluellen appeared. 'For God's sake, speak quietly, friend Gower,' he urged in a whisper. 'Why does no   25 one obey the ancient rules of war? If you studied the wars of Pompey the Great, you'd find there was no careless talk in his camp, I assure you.'

Gower protested that the French had been making a noise all night.

'If the enemy are noisy fools, must we be noisy fools also?' whispered Fluellen.

5   Gower promised Fluellen that he would speak more quietly and the two walked on.

Next appeared three ordinary English soldiers, walking around the camp to keep themselves warm.

'Is that the dawn, John Bates?' asked one called
10   Alexander Court, looking east.

'Yes,' said Bates, 'but we've no reason to welcome it.'

'We see the beginning of the day, but I think we'll never see the end of it,' declared Michael Williams, the third soldier. He stopped when he noticed a man in a
15   cloak, standing alone. 'Who goes there?'

'A friend,' Henry repeated.

'Which captain do you serve under?' asked Court.

'Sir Thomas Erpingham,' lied the king.

The king listens

20   The soldiers accepted him into their conversation.

'The king can show us all this courage,' said Bates, 'but, though the night's so cold, I think he'd rather be swimming in the River Thames than here. And I wish he was! And I wish I was with him!'

25   'I don't think the king wishes to be anywhere but where he is,' Henry said.

'Then I wish he was here on his own,' grumbled Bates. 'Because, if he was, he'd be ransomed and many poor men's lives would be saved.'

30   'Do you love the king so little?' asked Henry. 'I'd willingly die with him since his cause is just and his quarrel with France is honourable.'

'That's more than we know,' muttered Williams.

'Yes, and it's more than we need to know,' Bates declared. 'It's enough for us to know that we're the king's subjects and have to obey him. Then, if his cause is wrong, we can't be blamed.'

Williams said, 'But if his cause is wrong, the king will have a heavy debt to settle on the Day of Judgement when God punishes the wicked. All the people who die in battle today will cry for their injuries or their poor families. Few men die well in battle ...'

The three soldiers walked on, still arguing.

Henry sighed as they disappeared. 'Always the king! "Let us lay all our sins and responsibilities upon the king," people say. The king must bear all — and what does he get back? Just ceremony. Not even the good night's sleep enjoyed by every poor worker!'

Sir Thomas Erpingham returned to say that the nobles were worried by his absence.

Henry asked the knight to gather them all at his tent. Then, alone again for a few more moments, he began to pray: 'Oh, God of battles, put courage in my soldiers' hearts and let them not count the number of the enemy ... Oh, Lord, don't remember today, not today, what my father did to get the crown. I've buried King Richard's body at Westminster; I've built churches in memory of him; and I'll do more, I swear —'

The Duke of Gloucester approached, calling Henry's name. 'My brother?' said the king. 'I'm coming.'

The sun shines on the French

As the sun rose, the Constable and great dukes of France stood on the hillside above the French camp and ordered their horses to be brought to them.

'The sun shines on our armour! Up, my lords!' declared the Duke of Orleans.

'My horse! Bring me my horse! Together, we'll beat all, he and I!' boasted the Duke of Bourbon.

A messenger ran up, pointing at the valley below and announcing that the English were in their armour too.

'On your horses, great princes!' cried the Constable. He looked down into the valley and was scornful. 'What a poor, thin band of men! There's hardly enough blood in them for our weapons. Sound the trumpets!' At the approach of the French, he promised, the English would kneel in fear and surrender.

Lord Grandpre joined the dukes, asking what they were waiting for. 'Those wretched English are already on the field, careless of their own safety. Their flags hang sadly down. Their horsemen sit with torches in their hands, not moving; and their poor horses, with pale dead eyes and pale dull mouths, hang their heads, while the birds fly over them, waiting for their bones... It's hard to describe the life of anything so lifeless!'

'The English have said their prayers and now they wait for death,' the Constable agreed.

'Shall we send them food and fresh clothes before we fight with them?' laughed Bourbon.

'To the field now!' ordered the Constable. 'The sun is up. We're wasting time!'

Saint Crispin's Day

The English were counting the French army, as Henry had prayed they would not.

'There are 60,000 fighting men!' the Earl of Warwick reported in horror to the Duke of Exeter.

Exeter looked at the earl, his face serious. 'That's five to one,' he said. 'And they're all fresh.'

Warwick remembered that it was Saint Crispin's Day, a holiday in England. 'I wish 10,000 of those men not

working today in England were here with us in France!'
he muttered.

The king, who had ridden forward to study the
enemy, heard the earl's words as he returned. 'Don't
wish that, Warwick,' he said quickly. 'If we die, we're
enough men for our country to lose. And if we live,
then the greater share of honour each of us will have.
No, don't wish for one man more from England!'

He looked at all the nobles gathered together there,
waiting for his orders. 'Today is the Feast of Saint
Crispin,' he declared. 'He who fights with us and lives
through this day and comes safely home will be a proud
man each time he hears the name of Crispin. Each year
at this time, he'll feast his neighbours and roll up his
sleeve and say, "I got these wounds on Crispin's Day ..."
Old men forget, but he'll not forget the deeds he did
this day. He'll repeat our names and drink to the
memory of Harry the king, of Lancaster and Gloucester
and Clarence, of Exeter and you, my Earl of Warwick ...
Every good man will teach the story of this battle to his
son; and from this day to the end of the world
we few, we happy few, we band of
brothers will be remembered.'

Henry's eyes flashed.
'Gentlemen now in bed in
England,' he exclaimed,
'will curse themselves
that they weren't
here!'

Working warriors

A messenger arrived to say that the French were lined up, in handsome armour, flags flying and ready to charge.

5　'We're ready for them,' declared King Henry. 'You don't still wish for more help from England, Warwick?'

'My lord, I wish you and I could fight this royal battle alone!' replied Warwick boldly.

'That's better!' exclaimed Henry. 'My lords, you know
10　your places. God be with you all.'

A trumpet sounded and Montjoy, the French herald, approached. He had come once more, he said, to ask about a ransom.

'Who sent you this time?'

15　'The Constable of France.'

Then Henry told the herald to take back the same answer as before. Some of his men would die in the coming battle, he admitted, but many would return home to England with battle honours.

20　'Tell your Constable we're just ordinary working warriors, dirty from marching in the wind and rain. But, by God, our hearts are bright. And before night, my soldiers tell me, they'll be wearing clean new coats, that they have taken from the defeated French... Don't
25　come again for ransom,' the king ordered Montjoy. 'You'll get no ransom except my poor body. Tell that to the Constable.'

The herald departed and the Duke of York, Henry's cousin, knelt before the king, begging to be allowed to
30　lead the English into battle.

'Brave York!' Henry rode towards his army. 'The Duke of York will lead you forwards,' he shouted. 'March away, my soldiers! We're in God's hands now.'

11

HENRY THE FIFTH: THE BATTLE OF AGINCOURT

The battle begins

And so, on 25th October, the battle began. The French
charged into the valley on their fine horses — and the
English, though so weak and few in number, were not
immediately defeated. As the day went on, thousands   5
of Frenchmen were killed.

'The devil is in these English!' cried the Constable of
France in despair. 'Our ranks are broken.'

'We're shamed!' cried the Duke of Bourbon. 'Is this
the wretched enemy we laughed at?'   10

'Is this the king we asked for a ransom?' asked the
astonished Duke of Orleans. 'The day is lost!'

The Constable said the situation was hopeless. But
there were still more French than English on the
battlefield — enough to win, Orleans thought, if they   15
could get back into any sort of order.

'Order? It's too late for order now!' cried Bourbon
wildly. 'I'll lead another charge. A short life is better
than shame for ever!' And he rode back into the valley.

In the fighting, even Pistol captured a French soldier.   20
'What is your name?' he roared.

'Seigneur Dieu!' cried the Frenchman in fear. The
words meant 'Lord God' but Pistol did not know that.

'This Lord Dew must be a gentleman!' declared Pistol,
and demanded a ransom. 'Tell him in French,' he   25
ordered the boy, 'that unless he pays me, I'll cut his
throat with my sword.'

The boy explained this to the Frenchman, who knelt
at Pistol's feet, begging for mercy and promising money.

'Then inform him that my anger has disappeared and I'll accept his ransom.'

'He thanks you a thousand times for saving his life,' the boy told Pistol, 'and thinks you are the bravest, most worthy lord in England.'

'Follow me!' Pistol ordered his prisoner and marched away proudly.

'Talk, all talk!' the boy muttered. 'Even Bardolph and Nim had more courage, and they're both hanged — as this one would be if he was brave enough to steal anything!' He did not follow: it was his job now to help guard the camp. 'The French could do well if they came,' he thought. 'There's no one guarding the supplies except us boys.'

Anger against the French

By this time, the English had taken many French prisoners, but the French had not surrendered and soon there was the sound of trumpets and another charge.

'The French have pulled their men together. Tell all our soldiers to kill their prisoners,' Henry ordered the Duke of Exeter.

Pistol heard the king's command with despair. If he killed his prisoner, he would lose the promised ransom money. He hesitated. He looked at the prisoner. Then, in obedience to the king, he cut his throat...

The French made another charge, led by the Duke of Bourbon.

Some of them also entered the English camp and killed the boys guarding it.

'To kill the boys! That's against the rules of war!' exclaimed Fluellen, shaking his head in horror.

'Not a boy left alive,' said Gower. 'It's the cowards who ran away from the battle who've done it. They've

burned everything in the king's tent too. He was right
to order every soldier to cut his prisoner's throat. He's
a good king!'

'Yes, he was born in Wales,' replied Fluellen proudly.

Trumpets sounded. More French prisoners were led   5
past, including the dukes of Bourbon and Orleans.

Henry learned of the murder of the boys and was
angry for the first time, he said, since he arrived in
France. He noticed some French lords watching from
the hillside. 'Ride up to those horsemen,' he ordered a   10
messenger. 'Tell them either to come down and fight
or to get out of our sight. If they do neither, say we'll
cut the throat of every new French prisoner too —'

Montjoy, the French herald, appeared.

'What's the meaning of this, herald?' Henry demanded.   15
'You've not come again for a ransom?'

The herald shook his head. The French just asked,
he said, to be permitted to record and bury their dead.
Their princes and ordinary soldiers lay drowned in
blood together, still being kicked by their wounded   20
horses. 'Allow us, great king,' he begged, 'to sort our
nobles from our common men and bury the bodies.'

Victory for England

'But have the French surrendered?' Henry asked. 'They
still have horsemen on the field.'   25

'You've won the battle,' Montjoy answered.

'God be praised!' the king exclaimed in joy. 'What is
that castle over there?' The herald said it was Agincourt.
'Then we'll call this the Battle of Agincourt, fought on
Saint Crispin's Day,' announced the king.   30

'Your great-uncle Edward, the Black Prince of Wales,
also fought bravely here in France, Your Majesty,' said
Fluellen.

'He did,' Henry agreed. 'And the Welsh did good service in a place where leeks grew, and we still wear leeks in our caps in memory of it. I believe Your Majesty himself wears a leek on our Saint David's Day?'

'I do, for I am Welsh like you, good Fluellen,' Henry smiled.

'Yes, you are a true Welshman!' declared Fluellen.

Henry sent an English messenger with Montjoy to bring back exact numbers of the dead. When the messenger returned, he handed the king a long list.

Henry looked at it. 'This paper tells of 10,000 French lying dead on the battlefield!' he exclaimed. 'And it names 126 princes and nobles. Where is the number of our English dead?'

The messenger gave Henry a second, very short list.

The king read it, astonished. 'Only four noble names! "The Duke of York, the Earl of Suffolk, Sir Richard Keighley and Davy Gam, gentleman." And just twenty-five other English dead. Was there ever before such a great loss on one side, and so little loss on the other? God fought with us. The glory is His alone.'

The Duke of Exeter told him that they had also taken prisoner 1,500 French lords and knights, including the dukes of Bourbon and Orleans.

'Come, uncle,' said the king. 'Let us give thanks to God and bury our dead. Then we'll leave for England.'

Pistol finds Fluellen

In London, Henry was greeted like a conquering hero by the citizens, though he refused to have a victory procession, saying the victory was God's alone.

But the French king did not surrender his throne and, although the Dauphin Louis died and the Holy Roman Emperor tried to make peace between the two kingdoms, the war went on.   5

The English army laid siege to the towns of northern France — and on Saint David's Day, Pistol found Captain Fluellen wearing a leek in his cap. So Pistol brought the Welshman bread and salt, and told him to eat his Welsh vegetable …   10

'Why are you still wearing your leek?' Captain Gower asked Fluellen the next day. 'Saint David's Day is over.'   15

'I'm wearing it, my friend,' Fluellen replied, 'until I see that boastful knave Pistol again. Yesterday he told me to eat my leek!'

At that moment, Pistol came along.

'You rotten knave,' said Fluellen, taking the leek from his cap, 'I beg you to eat this leek. Your stomach doesn't like it, so I wish you to eat it.'   20

'Not even for Saint David,' declared Pistol.

'Eat it, knave,' ordered Fluellen, and hit him on the head with a stick.   25

'Base Welshman, you'll die for this!' roared Pistol.

'I'll die when God chooses,' replied Fluellen. 'In the meantime, you'll eat this leek. Come, here's sauce to go with it,' and he hit Pistol again. 'Bite.'

'By this leek, I shall take horrible revenge!' shouted Pistol. But Fluellen threatened him again with the stick, and he began to eat.   30

'More sauce, knave?' asked Fluellen. 'I pray you, throw nothing away. That skin will help mend your broken head.' The two captains waited until Pistol had eaten all the leek, then departed.

Pistol sighed. Fortune had turned against him. 'My Doll Tearsheet has died. I grow old. My honour has been beaten out of me,' he said sadly. Then he brightened. 'I'll go back to England and learn how to steal! I'll bandage these wounds, and swear I got them in the French wars...'

Henry meets Katherine

Still the fighting continued and France suffered. Finally, one of its most powerful dukes, the Duke of Burgundy, was able to bring the French and English kings face to face. Henry came to the French court, near Paris, and was greeted by King Charles with his queen, Isabel and daughter, Katherine.

The English had given the French a list of their demands. Charles was eager for peace and he retired to study the demands with Burgundy and Henry's advisers.

Henry, at his request, was left alone with the lovely Princess Katherine and her lady-in-waiting, Alice. He had given up his immediate claim to the French throne, but marriage with Katherine was the first of his demands, because such a marriage would make the claim twice as strong.

Katherine, however, could still speak little English. 'Your Majesty will laugh at me,' she said slowly. 'I cannot speak your England!'

'If you will love me with a whole heart, I'll not laugh at your bad English,' Henry promised. 'Do you like me, Kate?'

'Excuse me?' the princess replied, looking at Alice for help. 'I cannot tell what is "like me".'

'A goddess is like you, Kate, and you are like a goddess,' Henry replied, and Alice repeated his words in French. 'But I can only speak to you as a plain soldier,' he protested. 'I can't use these lovers' words — yet I do love you. Can you love me?'   5

'Is it possible that I should love the enemy of France?' she asked.

'No!' the King of England cried. 'But if you love me, you'll love the friend of France, for I love France so well that I'll not give up one village of it!'   10

The princess said she did not understand.

Henry tried to explain in French, then stopped, saying his French was as poor as her English. 'Kate, do you understand this much English? C-a-n y-o-u l-o-v-e m-e?'   15

'I cannot tell,' she said with a little smile.

Love and peace

The king looked in despair at Alice. 'Then can any of your friends tell? Come, I'm sure you love me, and I love you, and between us we'll produce a warrior son,   20 half French, half English, to conquer Constantinople! So, the most beautiful Katherine in the world, will you have me? As soon as you say "Harry of England, I am yours," then I'll say "England and Ireland and France are yours, and Harry Plantagenet is yours". So, Katherine, queen   25 of all, tell me in your bad English, will you have me?'

'If it will please my father, the king,' she answered, 'it will also please me.'

'Oh, it will please him, Kate!' Henry declared. 'So let me kiss your hand and —'   30

'No!' Katherine stepped back. Henry was her lord, she said. He must not bend to kiss her hand.

'Then I'll kiss your lips, Kate.' Henry moved closer.

'*Non, non!*' In a flood of French, the princess and her lady-in-waiting protested that French ladies were never kissed before their wedding. But Henry kissed Katherine anyway, and she allowed him to...

'You're teaching our princess English, Your Majesty?' laughed Burgundy as the court returned.

'She's learning how much I love her,' Henry replied. 'Shall Kate be my wife?'

'Yes,' said King Charles. He had agreed to all the English demands. He would sign a treaty. He would even name Henry as the next King of France. 'Marry my fair daughter Katherine,' Charles told him, 'and may your children bring our two kingdoms together at last in love and peace.'

Henry kissed the princess again, this time as his queen.

The trumpets sounded joyfully and Queen Isabel blessed the pair. 'May God join your two hearts as one, and your two kingdoms as one,' she smiled.

'Then prepare for our wedding day,' Henry declared, 'and let the peace treaty be signed.'

And so, in 1420, the peace treaty was signed and Henry the Fifth of England married Katherine of France. But Henry died two years later and, although Henry and Katherine's son, Henry the Sixth, was crowned King of England and France, the war between the two kingdoms continued.

QUESTIONS AND ACTIVITIES

CHAPTER 1

Use these words to fill in the gaps and say who was related to whom: **grandfather**, **grandson**, **father**, **brother**, **cousin**, **nephew**.

1 Henry Bolingbroke was a _grandson_ of King Edward the Third.

2 Harry Percy was the _nephew_ of the Earl of Worcester.

3 John of Gaunt was the _father_ of Harry, Prince of Wales.

4 The Earl of Northumberland was Hotspur's _father_, and _brother_ of the Earl of Worcester.

5 Henry Bolingbroke was a _cousin_ of Richard the Second.

CHAPTER 2

Put the words in the last part of these sentences in the right order.

1 As the thieves were emptying the purses, [and] [back] [Poins] [attacked] [prince] [the] [and] [them] [came].

2 Bardolph pushed stiff grass [to] [bleed] [it] [up] [make] [nose] [his].

3 In the play, Falstaff used the large chair for his [cushion] [for] [and] [his] [throne] [crown] [the].

4 On Harry's orders, Bardolph emptied [pockets] [tavern] [knight's] [bill] [out] [a] [the] [and] [read].

CHAPTER 3

Put the underlined sentences in the right paragraphs.

1 (a) Glendower, Northumberland and Hotspur were dividing England between them. (b) <u>The king admitted the great debt</u>

he owed to the Percys. (c) His share wasn't as large as the other two.

2 (a) Henry the Fourth was very angry with his eldest son, Harry. (b) But Hotspur did not like the division. (c) Then he began to answer, begging his father to forgive him for the faults of youth.

3 (a) Sir Walter Blunt came to the rebels with a message from King Henry. (b) Harry listened to his father almost in silence. (c) He was willing to settle any arguments, and to pardon them and all the other rebels.

CHAPTER 4

Some of these sentences are true, and some are false. Which are the true ones? What is wrong with the false ones?

F **1** The Prince of Wales refused to fight in a battle against Hotspur.

T **2** Hotspur's uncle lied about the king's offer of a pardon.

T **3** The Earl of Douglas believed that he had killed the king.

T **4** Two of King Henry's sons fought in the Battle of Shrewsbury.

F **5** Falstaff was killed by the Earl of Douglas.

CHAPTER 5

*Use these words to fill in the gaps: **called**, **come**, **king**, **knight**, **prince**, **service**, **street**, **deaf**, **action**, **pardoned**.*

When the Lord Chief Justice (1) _called_ to Falstaff in the (2) _street_, Falstaff's page said that Falstaff was (3) _deaf_. When he was forced to speak, Falstaff tried to discuss the (4) _king_ instead of himself. The Chief Justice asked Falstaff why he had not (5) _come_ to see him. Falstaff said he had been on military (6) _service_. The justice said that Falstaff's service at Shrewsbury meant his (7) _action_ at Gad's Hill could be (8) _pardoned_. He warned the (9) _prince_ not to be a bad influence on the (10) _knight_

CHAPTER 6

*Who said these things? Choose from: **the Earl of Westmoreland**, **Prince Harry**, **Prince John**, **Falstaff**, **Mistress Quickly**, **Doll Tearsheet**, **Pistol**.*

1 'Lord, how old men do lie!' Falstaff
2 'You're as brave as the great hero, Hector of Troy!' Doll
3 'You should be a man of peace, Your Grace.' the Earl
4 'Good health to you, my Lord of York!' Prince John
5 'God bless your sweet face!' Mistress
6 'I'll see her damned first!' Pistol
7 'I could cut off his ears for this!' Prince Harry

CHAPTER 7

Put the beginning of each sentence with the right ending.

1 When the king did not seem to move or breathe, ...

(a) and his smile grew until it stretched right across his face.

2 When Harry realized his father still lived, he knelt beside him, ...

(b) must never be allowed to come within ten miles of him.

3 In 1413 Henry Bolingbroke died and Harry, his eldest son, ...

(c) held out the crown and begged to be forgiven.

4 When Falstaff heard that the king was dead, he began to smile, ...

(d) Harry lifted the crown from the pillow and put it on his own head.

5 Henry the Fifth told the Lord Chief Justice that Falstaff ...

(e) became Henry the Fifth, King of England.

CHAPTER 8

Put the letters of these words in the right order.

The archbishop told Henry the Fifth that he had a true (1) **malic** claim to the French throne. Then King Henry called in the French

(2) **bomasrasad**, who gave him a message from the
(3) **pahinud**, the son of the French king. He would not listen to
Henry's claims to any French (4) **mudsekod** instead he gave
him some (5) **nestin** balls as a present. After the meeting, the
English court went wild with (6) **tecetmixen**. England would go
to war with France!

CHAPTER 9

*Something is wrong in the underlined part of each sentence.
What should it be?*

1 The Duke of Exeter, <u>King Henry's nephew</u>, was ambassador
   to the French king at Rouen.
2 Henry surrounded Harfleur and urged his men <u>to destroy the
   town gates</u>.
3 The siege continued into September, <u>and then Henry gave
   up</u>.
4 The Dauphin's sister, Princess Katherine, <u>decided to learn
   sewing</u>, as she was to marry the English king.
5 On 24th October, Henry camped <u>within ten miles of the
   French</u> at Agincourt.

CHAPTER 10

*Put these sentences in the right order to say what this part
of the story is about. Start with number 3.*

1 The king joined in the conversation of the three soldiers.
2 The king allowed the Duke of York to lead the English army
   into battle.
3 The English and French armies were so close they could see
   each other's camps.
4 The English, already on the field, were counting the French
   army.
5 Henry the Fifth walked around the camp, visiting his men
   and encouraging them.
6 At sunrise, the French stood on the hillside above their camp.
7 Erpingham lent the king his cloak to use as a disguise.

CHAPTER 11

Correct the six errors to say what happened in the Battle of Agincourt.

The Battle of Agincourt was fought in 1415 on 24th October. The French army was much larger than the English one. The English army, though so weak and few in numbers, were immediately defeated. Even Pistol was captured by a French soldier. King Henry ordered his soldiers to ransom their prisoners. The Dauphin appeared before King Henry to announce that the English had won the battle. There were 100,000 French dead, including 126 princes and nobles. Only four nobles from the English army were still alive.

Oxford
Progressive
English Readers